On Right Livelihood

Also by J. Krishnamurti

On Right Livelihood

J. Krishnamurti

HarperSanFrancisco
A Division of HarperCollins*Publishers*

For additional information, write to:
Krishnamurti Foundation Trust Limited
Brockwood Park, Bramdean, Hants, England SO24 0LQ

or

Krishnamurti Foundation of America
P.O. Box 1560
Ojai, CA 93024, United States

Sources and acknowledgments can be found on page 173.

Series editor: Mary Cadogan

Associate editors: Ray McCoy and David Skitt

FIRST EDITION

Library of Congress Cataloging-in-Publication Data

Krishnamurti, J. (Jiddu)

   On right livelihood / J. Krishnamurti. — 1st ed.

      p.   cm.

   Includes bibliographical references.

   ISBN 0-06-250609-9 (alk. paper)

   1. Philosophy.   2. Vocation.   3. Work—Religious aspects.

   4. Conduct of life.   I. Title.

   B5134.K7530566 1992

   181'.4—dc20   91–55328
                                                                    CIP

92   93   94   95   96   ❖   MAL   10   9   8   7   6   5   4   3   2   1

This edition is printed on acid-free paper that meets the American National
Standards Institute Z39.48 Standard.

Is it not necessary for each one to know for himself what is the right means of livelihood? If we are avaricious, envious, seeking power, then our means of livelihood will correspond to our inward demands and so produce a world of competition, ruthlessness, oppression, ultimately ending in war.

Ojai, 9 July 1944

Contents

Foreword

JIDDU KRISHNAMURTI was born in India in 1895 and, at the age of thirteen, taken up by the Theosophical Society, which considered him to be the vehicle for the 'world teacher' whose advent it had been proclaiming. Krishnamurti was soon to emerge as a powerful, uncompromising, and unclassifiable teacher, whose talks and writings were not linked to any specific religion and were neither of the East nor the West but for the whole world. Firmly repudiating the messianic image, in 1929 he dramatically dissolved the large and monied organization that had been built around him and declared truth to be 'a pathless land', which could not be approached by any formalized religion, philosophy, or sect.

For the rest of his life he insistently rejected the guru status that others tried to foist upon him. He continued to attract large audiences throughout the world but claimed no authority, wanted no disciples, and spoke always as one individual to another. At the core of his teaching was the realization that fundamental changes in society can be brought about only by a transformation of individual consciousness. The need for self-knowledge and an understanding of the restrictive, separative influences of religious and nationalistic conditionings, was constantly stressed. Krishnamurti pointed always to the urgent need for openness, for that 'vast space in the brain in which there is unimaginable energy'. This seems to have been the wellspring of his own creativity and the key to his catalytic impact on such a wide variety of people.

He continued to speak all over the world until he died in 1986 at the age of ninety. His talks and dialogues, journals and letters have been collected into more than sixty books. From that vast body of teachings this series of theme books has been compiled. Each book focuses on an issue that has particular relevance to and urgency in our daily lives.

On Right Livelihood

Ojai, 9 July 1944

A SIMPLE LIFE does not consist merely in the possession of few things, but in right livelihood and in the freedom from distractions, addictions, and possessiveness. Freedom from acquisitiveness will create the means of right livelihood, but there are certain obvious wrong means. Greed, tradition, and the desire for power will bring about the wrong means of livelihood. Even in these times when everybody is harnessed to a particular kind of work, it is possible to find right occupation. Each one must become aware of the issues of wrong occupation with its disasters and miseries, weary routine and death-dealing ways. Is it not necessary for each one to know for himself what is the right means of livelihood? If we are avaricious, envious, seeking power, then our means of livelihood will correspond to our inward demands and so produce a world of competition, ruthlessness, oppression, ultimately ending in war.

Ojai, 3 June 1945

Questioner: The problem of earning a decent living is predominant with most of us. Since economic currents of the world are hopelessly interdependent I find that almost anything I do either exploits others or contributes to the cause of war. How is one who honestly wishes to achieve right means of livelihood to withdraw from the wheels of exploitation and war?

Krishnamurti: For one who truly wishes to find a right means of livelihood, economic life as at present organized is certainly difficult. As the questioner says, economic currents are interrelated and so it is a complex problem, and as with all complex human problems it must be approached with simplicity. As society is becoming more and more complex and organized, regimentation of thought and action is being enforced for the sake of efficiency. Efficiency becomes ruthlessness when sensory values predominate, when eternal value is set aside.

Obviously there are wrong means of livelihood. One who helps in manufacturing arms and other methods to kill his fellow man is surely occupied with furthering violence, which never brings about peace in the world. The politician who, either for the benefit of his nation or of himself or of an ideology, is occupied in ruling and exploiting others, is surely employing wrong means of livelihood, which leads to war, to the misery and sorrow of man. The priest who holds to a specialized prejudice, dogma, or belief, to a particular form of worship and prayer, is also using wrong means of livelihood, for he is only spreading ignorance and intolerance, which set man against man. Any profession that leads to and maintains the divisions and conflict between man and man is obviously a wrong means of livelihood. Such occupations lead to exploitation and strife.

Our means of livelihood are dictated, are they not, through tradition or through greed and ambition? Generally we do not deliberately set about choosing the right means of livelihood. We are only too thankful to get what we can, and blindly follow the economic system that is about us. But the questioner wants to know how to withdraw from exploitation and war. To withdraw from them he must not allow himself to be influenced, nor follow traditional occupation, nor must he be envious and ambitious. Many of us choose some profession because of tradition or because we are of a family of lawyers or soldiers or politicians or traders; or our greed for power and position dictates our occupation; ambition drives us to compete and be ruthless in our desire to succeed. So one who would not exploit or contribute to the cause of war must cease to follow tradition, cease to be greedy, ambitious, self-seeking. If he abstains from these he will naturally find right occupation.

Although it is important and beneficial, right occupation is not an end in itself. You may have a right means of livelihood, but if you are inwardly insufficient and poor you will be a source of misery to yourself and so to others; you will be thoughtless, violent, self-assertive. Without the inward freedom of reality you will have no joy, no peace. In the search and discovery of that inward reality alone can we be not only content with little, but aware of something that is beyond all measure. It is this that must be sought out first, then other things will come into being in its wake.

This inward freedom of creative reality is not a gift; it is to be discovered and experienced. It is not an acquisition to be gathered to yourself to glorify yourself. It is a state of being, as silence, in which there is no becoming, in which there is completeness. This creativeness may not necessarily seek expression; it is not a talent that demands an outward manifestation. You need not be a great artist nor have an audience; if you seek these you will miss that inward reality. It is neither a gift, nor is it the outcome of talent; it is to be found, this imperishable treasure, when thought frees itself from lust, ill will, and ignorance, when thought frees itself from worldliness and personal craving to be. It is to be experienced through right thinking and meditation. Without this inward freedom of reality, existence is pain. As a thirsty man seeks water, so must we seek. Reality alone can quench the thirst of impermanency.

Ojai, 27 May 1945

WE HAVE OVER-DEVELOPED the intellect at the cost of our deeper and clearer feelings, and a civilisation that is based on the cultivation of the intellect must bring about ruthlessness and the worship of success. The emphasis on intellect or on emotion leads to unbalance, and intellect is ever seeking to safeguard itself. Mere determination only strengthens the intellect and blunts and hardens it; it is ever self-aggressive in becoming or not-becoming. The ways of the intellect must be understood through constant awareness and its re-education must transcend its own reasoning.

Questioner: I find there is conflict between my occupation and my relationship. They go in different directions. How can I make them meet?

Krishnamurti: Most of our occupations are dictated by tradition, or by greed, or by ambition. In our occupation we are ruthless, competitive, deceitful, cunning, and highly self-protective. If we weaken at any time, we may go under, so we must keep up with the high efficiency of the greedy machine of business. It is a constant struggle to maintain a hold, to become sharper and cleverer. Ambition can never find lasting satisfaction; it is ever seeking wider fields for self-assertiveness.

But in relationship quite a different process is involved. In it there must be affection, consideration, adjustment, self-denial, yielding, not to conquer but to live happily. In it there must be self-effacing tenderness, freedom from domination, from possessiveness, but emptiness and fear breed jealousy and pain in relationship. Relationship is a process of self-discovery, in which there is wider and deeper understanding. Relationship is a constant adjustment in self-discovery; it demands patience, infinite pliability, and a simple heart.

But how can the two meet together, self-assertiveness and love, occupation and relationship? The one is ruthless, competitive, ambitious, the other is self-denying, considerate, gentle; they cannot come together. With one hand people deal in blood and money, and with the other they try to be kind, affectionate, thoughtful. As a relief from their thoughtless and dull occupations they seek comfort and ease in relationship. But relationship does not yield comfort for it is a distinctive process of self-discovery and understanding. The man of occupation tries to seek through his life of relationship comfort and pleasure as a compensation for his wearisome business. His daily occupation of ambition, greed, and ruthlessness leads step by step to war and to the barbarities of modern civilisation.

Right occupation is not dictated by tradition, greed, or ambition. If each one is seriously concerned in establishing right relationship, not only with one but with all, then he will find right occupation. Right occupation comes with regeneration, with the change of heart, not with the mere intellectual determination to find it.

Integration is possible only if there is clarity of understanding on all the different levels of our consciousness. There can be no integration of love and ambition, deception and clarity, compassion and war. So long as occupation and relationship are kept apart, so long will there be endless conflict and misery. All reformation within the pattern of duality is retrogression; only beyond it, is there creative peace.

Bangalore, 8 August 1948

Questioner: You speak so much about the need for ceaseless alertness. I find my work dulls me so irresistibly that to talk of alertness after a day's work is merely putting salt on the wound.

Krishnamurti: Sir, this is an important question. Please let us examine it together carefully and see what it involves. Now most of us are dulled by what we call our work, the job, the routine. Those who love work, and those who are forced to work out of necessity and who see that work makes them dull—they are both dull. Both those who love their work and those who resist it are made dull, are they not? What does a man who loves his work do? He thinks about it from morning to night, he is constantly occupied with it. He is so identified with his work that he cannot look at it—he is himself the action, the work. And to such a person what happens? He lives in a cage, he lives in isolation with his work. In that isolation he may be very clever, very inventive, very subtle, but still he is isolated. And he is made dull because he is resisting all other work, all other approaches. His work is therefore a form of escape from life—from his wife, from his social duties, from innumerable demands, and so on. And there is the man in the other category, the man who—like most of you—is compelled to do something he dislikes and who resists it. He is the factory worker, the bank clerk, the lawyer, or whatever our various jobs are.

Now what is it that makes us dull? Is it the work itself? Or is it our resistance to work, or our avoidance of other impacts upon us? Do you follow the point? I hope I am making it clear. That is, the man who loves his work is so enclosed in it, so enmeshed, that it becomes an addiction. Therefore his love of work is an escape from life. And for the man who resists work, who wishes he were doing something else, there is the ceaseless conflict of resistance to what he is doing. So our problem is: Does work make the mind dull? Or is dullness brought about by resistance to work on the one hand, and by the use of work to avoid the impacts of life on the other? That is, does action, work, make the mind dull, or is the mind made dull by avoidance, by conflict, by resistance? Obviously, it is not work, but resistance, that dulls the mind. If you have no resistance and accept work, what happens? The work does not make you dull, because only a part of your mind is working with the job that you have to do. The rest of your being, the unconscious, the hidden, is occupied with those thoughts in which you are really interested. So there is no conflict. This may sound rather complex, but if you will carefully follow it you will see that the mind is made dull, not by work, but by resistance to work, or by resistance to life. Say, for example, you have to do a certain piece of work that may take five or six hours. If you say, 'What a bore, what an awful thing, I wish I could be doing something else', obviously your mind is resisting that work. Part of your mind is wishing you were doing something else. This division, brought about through resistance, creates dullness, because you are using your effort wastefully, wishing you were doing something else. Now if you do not resist it, but do what is actually necessary, then you say, 'I have to earn my livelihood and I will earn that livelihood rightly.' But right livelihood does not mean the army, the police, or being a lawyer who thrives on contention, disturbance, cunning subterfuge, and so on. This is quite a difficult problem in itself.

If you are occupied in doing something that you have to do to earn your livelihood, and if you resist it, obviously the mind becomes dull because that very resistance is like running an engine with the brake on. What happens to the poor engine? Its performance becomes dull, does it not? If you have driven a car, you know what will happen if you keep putting on the brake—you will not only wear out the brake, but you will wear out the engine. That is exactly what you are doing when you resist work. Whereas if you accept what you have to do, and do it as intelligently and as fully as possible, then what happens? Because you are no longer resisting, the other layers of your consciousness are active irrespective of what you are doing; you are giving only the conscious mind to your work, and the unconscious, the hidden part of your mind is occupied with other things in which there is much more vitality, much more depth. Though you face the work, the unconscious takes over and functions.

Now, if you observe, what actually happens in your daily life? You are interested, say, in finding God, in having peace. That is your real interest with which your conscious as well as your unconscious mind is occupied—to find happiness, to find reality, to live rightly, beautifully, clearly. But you have to earn a livelihood; because there is no such thing as living in isolation—that which is, is in relationship. So, being interested in peace, and since your work in daily life interferes with that, you resist work. You say, 'I wish I had more time to think, to meditate, to practise the violin', or whatever. When you do that, when you merely resist the work you have to do, that very resistance is a waste of effort, which makes the mind dull. But, if you realize that we all do various things that have to be done—writing letters, talking, clearing away the cow dung, or what you will—and therefore don't resist, but say, 'I have to do that work', then you will do it willingly and without boredom. If there is no resistance, the moment that work is over, you will find that the mind is peaceful; because the unconscious, the deeper layers of the mind are interested in peace, you will find that peace begins to come. So there is no division between action, which may be routine, which may be uninteresting, and your pursuit of reality; they are compatible when the mind is no longer resisting, when the mind is no longer made dull through resistance. It is the resistance that creates the division between peace and action. Resistance is based on an idea, and resistance cannot bring about action. It is only action that liberates, not the resistance to work.

So it is important to understand that the mind is made dull through resistance, through condemnation, blame, and avoidance. The mind is not dull when there is no resistance; when there is no blame, no condemnation, then it is alive, active. Resistance is merely isolation, and the mind of a man who consciously or unconsciously is continually isolating himself is made dull by this resistance.

Ojai, 14 August 1955

Questioner: You say that an occupied mind cannot receive that which is truth or God. But how can I earn a livelihood unless I am occupied with my work? Are you yourself not occupied with these talks as your particular means of earning a livelihood?

Krishnamurti: God forbid that I should be occupied with my talks! I am not. And this is not my means of livelihood. If I were occupied, there would be no interval between thoughts, there would not be that silence that is essential to see something new. Then talking would become utter boredom. I don't want to be bored by my own talks, therefore I am not talking from memory. It is something totally different. It doesn't matter, we shall go into that some other time.

The questioner asks how he is to earn his livelihood if he is not occupied with his work. Do you occupy yourself with your work? Please listen to this. If you are occupied with your work, then you do not love your work. Do you understand the difference? If I love what I am doing, I am not occupied with it, my work is not apart from me. But we are trained in this country, and unfortunately it is becoming the habit throughout the world, to acquire skill in work that we don't love. There may be a few scientists, a few technical experts, a few engineers, who really love what they do in the total sense of the word, which I am going to explain presently. But most of us do not love what we are doing, and that is why we are occupied with our livelihood. I think there is a difference between the two.

   If you really go into it, how can I love what I am doing if I am all the time driven by ambition, trying through my work to achieve an aim, to become somebody, to have success? An artist who is concerned with his name, with his greatness, with comparison, with fulfilling his ambition, has ceased to be an artist; he is merely a technician like everybody else. Which means, really, that to love something there must be a total cessation of all ambition, of all desire for the recognition of society—which is rotten anyhow. (Laughter.) Sirs, please don't. And we are not trained for that, we are not educated for that; we have to fit into some groove that society or the family has given us. Because my forefathers have been doctors, lawyers, or engineers, I must be a doctor, a lawyer, or an engineer. And now there must be more and more engineers, because that is what society demands. So we have lost this love of the thing itself— if we ever had it, which I doubt. When you love a thing, there is no occupation with it. The mind isn't conniving to achieve something, trying to be better than somebody else; all comparison, competition, all desire for success, for fulfilment, totally ceases. It is only the ambitious mind that is occupied.

   Similarly, a mind that is occupied with God, with truth, can never find it, because that which the mind is occupied with, it already knows. If you already know the immeasurable, what you know is the outcome of the past, therefore it is not the immeasurable. Reality cannot be measured, therefore there is no occupation with it. There is only a stillness of the mind, an emptiness in which there is no movement, and it is only then that the unknown can come into being.

From Commentaries on Living First Series, *Chapter 88*

Work

ALOOF AND INCLINED to be cynical, he was some kind of minister in the government. He had been brought along, or more probably dragged, by a friend, and seemed rather surprised at finding himself there. The friend wanted to talk something over and evidently thought that the other might as well come along and hear his problem. The minister was curious and rather superior. He was a big man, sharp of eye and a facile talker. He had arrived in life and was settling back. To travel is one thing, and to arrive is another. Travelling is constant arriving, and arrival that has no further travelling is death. How easily we are gratified, and how quickly discontent finds contentment! We all want a refuge of some kind, a haven from all conflict, and we generally find it. The clever, like the foolish, find their haven and are alert within it.

'I have been trying to understand my problem for a number of years, but I haven't been able to get to the bottom of it. In my work I have always brought about antagonism; enmity has somehow crept in among all the people I have tried to help. In helping some, I sow opposition among others. With one hand I give, and with the other I seem to injure. This has been going on for more years than I can remember, and now a situation has arisen in which I have to act rather decisively. I really don't want to hurt anyone, and I am at a loss as to what to do.'

Which is more important: not to hurt, not to create enmity, or to do some piece of work?

'In the course of my work I do hurt others. I am one of those people who throw themselves into their work; if I undertake something, I want to see it through. I have always been that way. I think I am fairly efficient and I hate to see inefficiency. After all, if we undertake some kind of social work, we must go through with it, and those who are inefficient or slack, naturally get hurt and become antagonistic. The work of bringing help to others is important, and in helping the needy I hurt those who come in the way. But I really don't want to hurt people, and I have begun to realize that I must do something about it.'

Which to you is important: to work, or not to hurt people?

'When one sees so much misery and plunges into the work of reform, in the course of that work one hurts certain people, though most unwillingly.'

In saving one group of people, others are destroyed. One country survives at the expense of another. The so-called spiritual people, in their ardour for reform, save some and destroy others; they bring blessings and also curses. We always seem to be kind to some and brutal to others. Why? Which to you is important: to work, or not to hurt people?

'After all, one has to hurt certain people, the slovenly, the inefficient, the selfish, it seems inevitable. Don't you hurt people by your talks? I know a rich man who has been very hurt by what you say about the wealthy.'

I do not want to hurt anyone. If people are hurt in the process of certain work, then to me that work has to be put aside. I have no work, no schemes for any kind of reform or revolution. With me work is not first, but not to hurt others. If the rich man feels hurt by what is said, he is not hurt by me, but by the truth of what is, which he dislikes; he doesn't want to be exposed. It is not my intention to expose another. If a man is temporarily exposed by the truth of what is and gets angry at what he sees, he puts the blame on others; but that is only an escape from the fact. It is foolish to be angry with a fact. Avoidance of a fact through anger is one of the commonest and most thoughtless reactions.

But you have not answered my question. Which to you is important: to work, or not to hurt people?

'Work has to be done, don't you think?' put in the minister.

Why should it be done? If in the course of benefiting some you hurt or destroy others, what value has it? You may save your particular country, but you exploit or maim another. Why are you so concerned about your country, your party, your ideology? Why are you so identified with your work? Why does work matter so much?

'We have to work, be active, otherwise we might as well be dead. When the house is burning, we cannot for the moment be concerned with fundamental issues.'

To the merely active, fundamentals are never the issue; they are only concerned with activity, which brings superficial benefits and deep harms. But, if I may ask, why is a certain kind of work so important to you? Why are you so attached to it?

'Oh, I don't know, but it gives me a great deal of happiness.'

So you are really not interested in the work itself, but in what you get out of it. You may not make money at it, but you derive happiness from it. As another gains power, position, and prestige in saving his party or his country, so you gain pleasure from your work; as another finds great satisfaction, which he calls a blessing, in serving his saviour, his guru, his Master, so you are satisfied by what you call altruistic work. Actually it is not the country, the work, or the saviour that is important to you, but what you get out of it. Your own happiness is all-important, and your particular work gives you what you want. You are really not interested in the people you are supposed to be helping; they are only a means to your happiness. And obviously the inefficient, those who stand in your way, get hurt; for the work matters, the work being your happiness. This is the brutal fact, but we cunningly cover it with high-sounding words like service, country, peace, God, and so on.

So, if one may point out, you really do not mind hurting people who hinder the efficiency of the work that gives you happiness. You find happiness in certain work, and that work, whatever it be, is you. You are interested in getting happiness, and the work offers you the means; therefore the work becomes very important, and then of course you are very efficient, ruthless, dominating for the sake of that which gives you happiness. So you do not mind hurting people, breeding enmity.

'I have never seen it that way before, and it is perfectly true. But what am I to do about it?'

Is it not important to find out also why you have taken so many years to see a simple fact like this?

'I suppose, as you say, I really didn't care whether I hurt people or not so long as I got my way. I generally do get my way, because I have always been very efficient and direct—which you would call ruthlessness, and you are perfectly right. But what am I to do now?'

You have taken all these years to see this simple fact because until now you have been unwilling to see it; for in seeing it you are attacking the very foundation of your being. You have sought happiness and found it, but it has always brought conflict and antagonism; and now, perhaps for the first time, you are facing facts about yourself. What are you going to do? Is there not a different approach to work? Is it not possible to be happy and work, rather than to seek happiness in work? When we use work or people as a means to an end, then obviously we have no relationship, no communion either with the work or with people; and then we are incapable of love. Love is not a means to an end; it is its own eternity. When I use you and you use me, which is generally called relationship, we are important to each other only as a means to something else; so we are not important to each other at all. From this mutual usage, conflict and antagonism must inevitably arise. So what are you going to do? Let us both discover what to do rather than seek an answer from another. If you can search it out, your finding of it will be your experiencing of it; then it will be real and not just a confirmation or conclusion, a mere verbal answer.

'What, then, is my problem?'

Can we not put it this way? Spontaneously, what is your first reaction to the question: Does the work come first? If it does not, then what does?

'I am beginning to see what you are trying to get at. My first response is shock; I am really appalled to see what I have been doing in my work for so many years. This is the first time I have faced the fact of what is, as you call it, and I assure you it is not very pleasant. If I can go beyond it, perhaps I shall see what is important, and then the work will naturally follow. But whether the work or something else comes first is still not clear to me.'

Why is it not clear? Is clarity a matter of time or of willingness to see? Will the desire not to see disappear by itself in the course of time? Is not your lack of clarity due to the simple fact that you don't want to be clear because it would upset the whole pattern of your daily life? If you are aware that you are deliberately postponing, are you not immediately clear? It is this avoidance that brings confusion.

'It is all becoming very clear to me now, and what I shall do is immaterial. Probably I shall do what I have been doing, but with quite a different spirit. We shall see.'

From The First and Last Freedom, *Chapter 3*

Individual and Society

A MIND THAT wishes to understand a problem must not only understand the problem completely, wholly, but must be able to follow it swiftly, because the problem is never static. The problem is always new, whether it is a problem of starvation, a psychological problem, or any problem. Any crisis is always new; therefore, to understand it a mind must always be fresh, clear, swift in its pursuit. I think most of us realize the urgency of an inward revolution, which alone can bring about a radical transformation of the outer, of society. This is the problem with which all seriously intentioned people are occupied. How to bring about a fundamental, a radical transformation in society, is our problem; and this transformation of the outer cannot take place without inner revolution. Since society is always static, any action, any reform that is accomplished without this inward revolution becomes equally static; so there is no hope without this constant inward revolution, because, without it, outer action becomes repetitive, habitual. The action of relationship between you and another, between you and me, is society; and that society becomes static, it has no life-giving quality, so long as there is not this constant inward revolution, a creative, psychological transformation. It is because there is not this constant inward revolution that society is always becoming static, crystallized, and has therefore constantly to be broken up.

What is the relationship between yourself and the misery, the confusion, in and around you? Surely this confusion, this misery, did not come into being by itself. You and I have created it, not a Capitalist nor a Communist nor a Fascist society, but you and I have created it in our relationship with each other. What you are within has been projected without, on to the world; what you are, what you think and what you feel, what you do in your everyday existence, is projected outwardly, and that constitutes the world. If we are miserable, confused, chaotic within, by projection that becomes the world, that becomes society, because the relationship between yourself and myself, between myself and another, is society—society is the product of our relationship—and if our relationship is confused, egocentric, narrow, limited, national, we project that and bring chaos into the world.

What you are, the world is. So your problem is the world's problem. Surely this is a simple and basic fact, is it not? In our relationship with the one or the many, we seem somehow to overlook this point all the time. We want to bring about alteration through a system or through a revolution in ideas or values based on a system, forgetting that it is you and I who create society, who bring about confusion or order by the way in which we live. So we must begin near; that is we must concern ourselves with our daily existence, with our daily thoughts and feelings and actions that are revealed in the manner of earning our livelihood and in our relationship with ideas or beliefs. This is our daily existence, is it not? We are concerned with livelihood, getting jobs, earning money; we are concerned with the relationship with our family or with our neighbours; and we are concerned with ideas and with beliefs.

Now, if you examine your occupation, it is fundamentally based on envy, it is not just a means of earning a livelihood. Society is so constructed that it is a process of constant conflict, constant becoming; it is based on greed, on envy—envy of your superior: the clerk wanting to become the manager, which shows that he is not just concerned with earning a livelihood, a means of subsistence, but with acquiring position and prestige. This attitude naturally creates havoc in society, in relationship, but if you and I were only concerned with livelihood we should find out the right means of earning it, a means not based on envy. Envy is one of the most destructive factors in relationship because envy indicates the desire for power, for position, and it ultimately leads to politics; both are closely related. The clerk, when he seeks to become a manager, becomes a factor in the creation of power-politics that produces war; so he is directly responsible for war.

WHY IS SOCIETY crumbling, collapsing, as it surely is? One of the fundamental reasons is that the individual—you—has ceased to be creative. I will explain what I mean. You and I have become imitative, we are copying, outwardly and inwardly. Outwardly, when learning a technique, when communicating with each other on the verbal level, naturally there must be some imitation, copy. I copy words. To become an engineer, I must first learn the technique, then use the technique to build a bridge. There must be a certain amount of imitation, copying, in outward technique, but when there is inward, psychological imitation, surely we cease to be creative. Our education, our social structure, our so-called religious life, are all based on imitation; that is, I fit into a particular social or religious formula. I have ceased to be a real individual; psychologically, I have become a mere repetitive machine with certain conditioned responses, whether of the Hindu, the Christian, the Buddhist, the German, or the Englishman. Our responses are conditioned according to the pattern of society, whether it is Eastern or Western, religious or materialistic. So one of the fundamental causes of the disintegration of society is imitation, and one of the disintegrating factors is the leader, whose very essence is imitation.

In order to understand the nature of disintegrating society is it not important to inquire whether you and I, the individual, can be creative? We can see that when there is imitation there must be disintegration, when there is authority there must be copying. And since our whole mental, psychological make-up is based on authority, there must be freedom from authority, to be creative. Have you not noticed that in moments of creativeness, those rather happy moments of vital interest, there is no sense of repetition, no sense of copying? Such moments are always new, fresh, creative, happy. So we see that one of the fundamental causes of the disintegration of society is copying, which is the worship of authority.

Bombay, 24 February 1957

Questioner: I am a student. Before I heard you I was keen about my studies and making a good career for myself. But now it all seems so futile, and I have completely lost interest in my studies and in a career. What you say seems very attractive, but it is impossible to attain. All this has left me very confused. What am I to do?

Krishnamurti: Sir, have I made you confused? Have I made you see that what you are doing is futile? If I have been the cause of your confusion, then you are not confused, because when I go away you will revert to your former confusion or your clarity. But if this questioner is serious, then what actually has taken place is that by listening to what has been said here he has awakened himself to his own activities; he now sees that what he is doing, studying to build up a career for the future, is rather empty, without much significance. So he says, 'What am I to do?' He is confused, not because I have made him confused, but because by listening he has become aware of the world situation and of his own condition and relationship with the world. He has become aware of the futility, the uselessness of all this business of building up a future career. He has become aware of it, I have not made him aware.

I think this is the first thing to realize: that by listening, by watching, by observing your own activities, you have made this discovery for yourself; therefore it is yours, not mine. If it were mine, I would take it away with me when I go. But this is something that cannot be taken away by another because it has been realized by you. You have watched yourself in action, you have observed your own life, and you now see that to build up a career for the future is a futile thing. So, being confused, you say, 'What am I to do?'

What are you to do, actually? You have to go on with your studies, have you not? That is obvious, because you have to have some kind of profession, a right means of livelihood. Do you understand? Please do listen to this. You have to earn a livelihood through a right means. And law is obviously not a right means, because it maintains society as it is, a society that is based on acquisitiveness, on greed, on envy, on authority and exploitation, and that is therefore in turmoil within itself. So law is not the profession for a man who is at all serious in religious matters; nor can he become a policeman or a soldier. Soldiering is obviously a profession of killing, and there is no difference between defence and offence. A soldier is prepared to kill, and the function of a general is to prepare for war.

So, if those three are not right professions, then what are you to do? You have to think it out, have you not? You have to find out for yourself what you really want to do, and not rely on your father, on your grandmother, on some professor, or on anybody else to tell you what to do. And what does it mean to find out what you really want to do? It means finding out what you love to do, does it not? When you love what you are doing, you are not ambitious, you are not greedy, you are not seeking fame, because that very love of what you are doing is totally sufficient in itself. In that love there is no frustration, because you are no longer seeking fulfilment.

But you see, all this demands a great deal of thinking, a great deal of inquiry, meditation, and unfortunately the pressure of the world is very strong—the world being your parents, your grandparents, the society around you. They all want you to be a successful man, they want you to fit into the established pattern, so they educate you to conform. But the whole structure of society is based on acquisitiveness, on envy, on ruthless self-assertion, on the aggressive activity of each one of us; and if you see for yourself, actually and not theoretically, that such a society must inevitably rot from within, then you will find your own way of action through doing what you love to do. It may produce a conflict with the present society—and why not? A religious man, or the man who is seeking truth, is in revolt against the society that is based essentially on respectability, acquisitiveness, and the ambitious search for power. He is not in conflict with society, but society is in conflict with him. Society can never accept him. Society can only make him a saint and worship him—and thereby destroy him.

So the student who has been listening is now confused. But if he does not escape from that confusion—by running off to a cinema, by going to a temple, by reading a book, or by turning to a guru—and realizes how his confusion has arisen, if he faces that confusion and in the process of inquiry does not conform to the pattern of society, then he will be a truly religious man. And such religious men are necessary for it is they who will bring about a new world.

From Commentaries on Living Second Series, *Chapter 31*

What Is the True Function of a Teacher?

THE BANYANS AND the tamarinds dominated the small valley, which was green and alive after the rains. In the open the sun was strong and biting, but in the shade it was pleasantly cool. The shadows were deep, and the old trees were shapely against the blue sky. There was an astonishing number of birds in that valley, birds of many different kinds, and they would come to these trees and so quickly disappear in them. There would probably be no more rain for several months but now the countryside lay green and peaceful, the wells were full, and there was hope in the land. The corrupting towns were far beyond the hills, but the nearby villages were filthy and the people were starving. The government only promised, and the villagers seemed to care so little. There was beauty and gladness all about them, but they had no eyes for it nor for their own inward riches. Amidst so much loveliness the people were dull and empty.

He was a teacher with little pay and a large family, but he was interested in education. He said he had a difficult time making ends meet, but he managed somehow, and poverty was not a disturbing factor. Though food was not in abundance, they had enough to eat, and as his children were being educated freely in the school where he was teaching, they could scrape along. He was proficient in his subject and taught other subjects too, which he said any teacher could do who was at all intelligent. He again stressed his deep interest in education.

'What is the function of a teacher?' he asked.

Is he merely a giver of information, a transmitter of knowledge?

'He has to be at least that. In any given society, boys and girls must be prepared to earn a livelihood, depending on their capacities, and so on. It is part of the function of a teacher to impart knowledge to the student so that he may have a job when the time comes, and may also, perhaps, help to bring about a better social structure. The student must be prepared to face life.'

That is so, sir, but aren't we trying to find out what is the function of a teacher? Is it merely to prepare the student for a successful career? Has the teacher no greater and wider significance?

'Of course he has. For one thing, he can be an example. By the way of his life, by his conduct, attitude, and outlook, he can influence and inspire the student.'

Is it the function of a teacher to be an example to the student? Are there not already enough examples, heroes, leaders, without adding another to the long list? Is example the way of education? Is it not the function of education to help the student to be free, to be creative? And is there freedom in imitation, in conformity, whether outward or inward? When the student is encouraged to follow an example, is not fear sustained in a deep and subtle form? If the teacher becomes an example, does not that very example mould and twist the life of the student, and are you not then encouraging the everlasting conflict between what he is and what he should be? Is it not the function of a teacher to help the student to understand what he is?

'But the teacher must guide the student towards a better and nobler life.'

To guide, you must know; but do you? What do you know? You know only what you have learned through the screen of your prejudices, which is your conditioning as a Hindu, a Christian, or a Communist; and this form of guidance only leads to greater misery and bloodshed, as is being shown throughout the world. Is it not the function of a teacher to help the student to free himself intelligently from all these conditioning influences so that he will be able to meet life deeply and fully, without fear, without aggressive discontent? Discontent is part of intelligence, but not the easy pacification of discontent. Acquisitive discontent is soon pacified, for it pursues the well-worn pattern of acquisitive action. Is it not the function of a teacher to dispel the gratifying illusion of guides, examples, and leaders?

'Then at least the teacher can inspire the student to greater things.'

Again, are you not approaching the problem wrongly, sir? If you as a teacher infuse thought and feeling into the student, are you not making him psychologically dependent on you? When you act as his inspiration, when he looks up to you as he would to a leader or to an ideal, surely he is depending on you. Does not dependence breed fear? And does not fear cripple intelligence?

'But if the teacher is not to be either an inspirer, an example, or a guide, then what in heaven's name is his true function?'

The moment you are none of those things, what are you? What is your relationship with the student? Did you previously have any relationship with the student at all? Your relationship with him was based on an idea of what was good for him, that he ought to be this or that. You were the teacher and he was the pupil; you acted upon him, you influenced him according to your particular conditioning so, consciously or unconsciously you moulded him in your own image. But if you cease to act upon him, then he becomes important in himself, which means that you have to understand him and not demand that he should understand you or your ideals, which are phony anyway. Then you have to deal with what is and not with what should be.

Surely when the teacher regards each student as a unique individual, and therefore not to be compared with any other, he is then not concerned with system or method. His sole concern is with 'helping' the student to understand the conditioning influences about him and within himself, so that he can face intelligently without fear, the complex process of living, and not add more problems to the already existing mess.

'Are you not asking of the teacher a task that is far beyond him?'

If you are incapable of this, then why be a teacher? Your question has meaning only if teaching is a mere career to you, a job like any other, for I feel that nothing is impossible for the true educator.

Varanasi, 12 January 1962

Questioner: After a day's hard work, one's mind gets tired. What is one to do?

Krishnamurti: The question is: After a day's work with so many occupations, one finds the little time that one has is occupied; the mind is weary; what is one to do?

You know, our whole social structure is all wrong; our education is absurd; our so-called education is merely repetition, memorizing, mugging up. How can a mind that has been struggling all day as a scientist, as a specialist, as this or that, that is so occupied for thirteen hours in something or other—how can it have a leisure that is fruitful? It cannot. How can you, after spending forty or fifty years as a scientist or a bureaucrat or a doctor or what you are—not that they are not necessary—have ten years when your mind is not conditioned, not incapable? So the question is really: Is it possible to go to the office, to be an engineer, to be an expert in fertilizers, to be a good educator, and yet, all day, every minute, keep the mind astonishingly sharp, sensitive, alive? That is really the issue, not how to have quietness at the end of the day. You are committed to engineering, to some specialization—you cannot help it, society demands it, and you have to go to work. Is it possible as you are working never to get caught in the wheels of the monstrous thing called society? I cannot answer for you. I say it is possible, not theoretically but actually. It is possible only when there is no centre;

that is why I was talking about it. Think of a doctor who is a nose and throat specialist, who has practised for fifty years. What is his heaven? His heaven is nose and throat obviously. But is it possible to be a good first-class doctor, and yet live, function, watch, be aware of the whole thing, of the whole process of thought? Surely it is possible, but that requires extraordinary energy. And that energy is wasted in conflict, in effort. That energy is wasted when you are vain, ambitious, envious.

We think of energy in terms of doing something, in terms of the so-called religious idea that you must have tremendous energy to reach God, and therefore you must be a bachelor, you must do this and do that—you know all the tricks that the religious people play upon themselves, and so end up half starved, empty, dull. God does not want dull people—the people who are insensitive. You can only go to God with complete aliveness, every part of you alive, vibrant; but you see, the difficulty is to live without falling into a groove, falling into habits of thought, of ideas, of action. If you apply your mind, you will find you can live in this ugly world—I am using the word *ugly* in the dictionary sense, without any emotional content behind it—and work and act, and at the same time keep the brain alert, like a river that purifies itself all the time.

From Commentaries on Living Second Series, *Chapter 17*

What Is Making You Dull?

HE HAD A small job, with a very poor salary; he came with his wife, who wanted to talk over their problem. They were both quite young, and though they had been married for some years, they had no children; but that was not the problem. His pay was barely enough to eke out an existence in these difficult times, but as they had no children it was sufficient to survive. What the future held no man knew, though it could hardly be worse than the present. He was disinclined to talk, but his wife pointed out that he must. She had brought him along, almost forcibly it appeared, for he had come very reluctantly; but there he was, and she was glad. He could not talk easily, he said, for he had never talked about himself to anyone but his wife. He had few friends, and even to these he never opened his heart, for they wouldn't have understood him. As he talked he was slowly thawing, and his wife was listening with anxiety. He explained that his work was not the problem; it was fairly interesting, and anyhow it gave them food. They were simple, unassuming people, and both had been educated at one of the universities.

At last she began to explain their problem. She said that for a couple of years now her husband seemed to have lost all interest in life. He did his office work, and that was about all; he went to work in the morning and came back in the evening, and his employers did not complain about him.

'My work is a matter of routine and does not demand too much attention. I am interested in what I do, but it is all somehow a strain. My difficulty is not at the office or with the people with whom I work, but it is within myself. As my wife said, I have lost interest in life, and I don't quite know what is the matter with me.'

'He was always enthusiastic, sensitive, and very affectionate, but for the past year or more he has become dull and indifferent to everything. He always used to be loving with me, but now life has become very sad for both of us. He doesn't seem to care whether I am there or not, and it has become a misery to live in the same house. He is not unkind or anything of that sort, but has simply become apathetic and utterly indifferent.'

Is it because you have no children?

'It isn't that', he said. 'Our physical relationship is all right, more or less. No marriage is perfect, and we have our ups and downs, but I don't think this dullness is the result of any sexual maladjustment. Although my wife and I haven't lived together sexually for some time now because of this dullness of mine, I don't think it is the lack of children that has brought it about.'

Why do you say that?

'Before this dullness came upon me, my wife and I realized that we couldn't have children. It has never bothered me, though she often cries about it. She wants children, but apparently one of us is incapable of reproduction. I have suggested several things that might make it possible for her to have a child, but she won't try any of them. She will have a child by me or not at all, and she is very deeply upset about it. After all, without the fruit, a tree is merely decorative. We have lain awake talking about all this, but there it is. I realize that one can't have everything in life, and it is not the lack of children that has brought on this dullness; at least, I am pretty sure it is not.'

Is it due to your wife's sadness, to her sense of frustration?

'You see, sir, my husband and I have gone into this matter pretty fully. I am more than sad not to have had children, and I pray to God that I may have one some day. My husband wants me to be happy, of course, but his dullness isn't due to my sadness. If we had a child now, I would be supremely happy, but for him it would merely be a distraction, and I suppose it is so with most men. This dullness has been creeping upon him for the past two years like some internal disease. He used to talk to me about everything, about the birds, about his office work, about his ambitions, about his regard and love for me; he would open his heart to me. But now his heart is closed and his mind is somewhere far away. I have talked to him, but it is no good.'

Have you separated from each other for a time to see how that worked?

'Yes. I went away to my family for about six months, and we wrote to each other; but this separation made no difference. If anything, it made things worse. He cooked his own food, went out very little, kept away from his friends, and was more and more withdrawn into himself. He has never been too social in any case. Even after this separation he showed no quickening spark.'

Do you think this dullness is a cover, a pose, an escape from some unfulfilled inner longing?

'I am afraid I don't quite understand what you mean.'

You may have an intense longing for something that needs fulfilment, and as that longing has no release, perhaps you are escaping from the pain of it through becoming dull.

'I have never thought about such a thing, it has never occurred to me before. How am I to find out?'

Why hasn't it occurred to you before? Have you ever asked yourself why you have become dull? Don't you want to know?

'It is strange, but I have never asked myself what is the cause of this stupid dullness. I have never put that question to myself.'

Now that you are asking yourself that question, what is your response?

'I don't think I have any. But I am really shocked to find how very dull I have become. I was never like this. I am appalled at my own state.'

After all, it is good to know in what state one actually is. At least that is a beginning. You have never before asked yourself why you are dull, lethargic; you have just accepted it and carried on, have you not? Do you want to discover what has made you like this, or have you resigned yourself to your present state?

'I am afraid he has just accepted it without ever fighting against it.'

You do want to get over this state, don't you? Do you want to talk without your wife?

'Oh, no. There is nothing I cannot say in front of her. I know it is not a lack or an excess of sexual relationship that has brought on this state, nor is there another woman. I couldn't go to another woman. And it is not the lack of children.'

Do you paint or write?

'I have always wanted to write, but I have never painted. On my walks I used to get some ideas, but now even that has gone.'

Why don't you try to put something on paper? It doesn't matter how stupid it is; you don't have to show it to anyone. Why don't you try writing something? But to go back. Do you want to find out what has brought on this dullness, or do you want to remain as you are?

'I would like to go away somewhere by myself, renounce everything, and find some happiness.'

Is that what you want to do? Then why don't you do it? Are you hesitating on account of your wife?

'I am no good to my wife as I am; I am just a wash-out.'

Do you think you will find happiness by withdrawing from life, by isolating yourself? Haven't you sufficiently isolated yourself now? To renounce in order to find is no renunciation at all; it is only a cunning bargain, an exchange, a calculated move to gain something. You give up this in order to get that. Renunciation with an end in view is only a surrender to further gain. But can you have happiness through isolation, through dissociation? Is not life association, contact, communion? You may withdraw from one association to find happiness in another, but you cannot completely withdraw from all contact. Even in complete isolation you are in contact with your thoughts, with yourself. Suicide is the complete form of isolation.

'Of course I don't want to commit suicide. I want to live, but don't want to continue as I am.'

Are you sure you don't want to go on as you are? You see, it is fairly clear that there is something that is making you dull, and you want to run away from it into further isolation. To run away from what is, is to isolate oneself. You want to isolate yourself, perhaps temporarily, hoping for happiness. But you have already isolated yourself, and pretty thoroughly; further isolation, which you call renunciation, is only a further withdrawal from life. And can you have happiness through deeper and deeper self-isolation? The nature of the self is to isolate itself; its very quality is exclusiveness. To be exclusive is to renounce in order to gain. The more you withdraw from association, the greater the conflict, resistance. Nothing can exist in isolation. However painful relationship may be, it has to be patiently and thoroughly understood. Conflict makes for dullness. Effort to become something only brings problems, conscious or unconscious. You cannot be dull without some cause, for, as you say, you were once alert and keen. You haven't always been dull. What has brought about this change?

'You seem to know, and won't you please tell him?'

I could, but what good would that be? He would either accept or reject it according to his mood and pleasure; but is it not important that he himself should find out? Is it not essential for him to uncover the whole process and see the truth of it? Truth is something that cannot be told to another. He must be able to receive it, and none can prepare him for it. This is not indifference on my part; but he must come to it openly, freely and unexpectedly.

What is making you dull? Shouldn't you know it for yourself? Conflict, resistance, makes for dullness. We think that through struggle we shall understand, through competition we shall be made bright. Struggle certainly makes for sharpness, but what is sharp is soon made blunt; what is in constant use soon wears out. We accept conflict as inevitable, and build our structure of thought and action upon this inevitability. But is conflict inevitable? Is there not a different way of living? There is if we can understand the process and significance of conflict.

Again, why have you made yourself dull?

'Have I made myself dull?'

Can anything make you dull unless you are willing to be made dull? This willingness may be conscious or hidden. Why have you allowed yourself to be made dull? Is there a deep-seated conflict in you?

'If there is, I am totally unaware of it.'

But don't you want to know? Don't you want to understand it?

'I am beginning to see what you are driving at', she put in, 'but I may not be able to tell my husband the cause of his dullness because I am not quite sure of it myself.'

You may or may not see the way this dullness has come upon him, but would you really be helping him if verbally you were to point it out? Is it not essential that he discovers it for himself? Please see the importance of this, and then you will not be impatient or anxious. One can help another, but he alone must undertake the journey of discovery. Life is not easy; it is very complex, but we must approach it simply. We are the problem; the problem is not what we call life. We can understand the problem, which is ourselves, only if we know how to approach it. The approach is all important, and not the problem.

'But what are we to do?'

You must have listened to all that has been said. If you have, then you will see that truth alone brings freedom. Please don't worry, but let the seed take root.

After some weeks they both came back. There was hope in their eyes and a smile upon their lips.

From This Matter of Culture, *Chapter 17*

I DON'T KNOW if on your walks you have noticed a long, narrow pool beside the river. Some fishermen must have dug it, and it is not connected with the river. The river is flowing steadily, deep and wide, but this pool is heavy with scum because it is not connected with the life of the river, and there are no fish in it. It is a stagnant pool, and the deep river, full of life and vitality, flows swiftly along.

Now, don't you think human beings are like that? They dig a little pool for themselves away from the swift current of life, and in that little pool they stagnate, die; and this stagnation, this decay we call existence. That is, we all want a state of permanency; we want certain desires to last forever, we want pleasures to have no end. We dig a little hole and barricade ourselves in it with our families, with our ambitions, our cultures, our fears, our gods, our various forms of worship, and there we die, letting life go by—that life which is impermanent, constantly changing, which is so swift, which has such enormous depths, such extraordinary vitality and beauty.

Have you not noticed that if you sit quietly on the banks of the river you hear its song—the lapping of the water, the sound of the current going by? There is always a sense of movement, an extraordinary movement towards the wider and the deeper. But in the little pool there is no movement at all, its water is stagnant. And if you observe you will see that this is what most of us want: little stagnant pools of existence away from life. We say that our pool-existence is right, and we have invented a philosophy to justify it; we have developed social, political, economic, and religious theories in support of it, and we don't want to be disturbed because, you see, what we are after is a sense of permanency.

Do you know what it means to seek permanency? It means wanting the pleasurable to continue indefinitely and wanting that which is not pleasurable to end as quickly as possible. We want the name that we bear to be known and to continue through family, through property. We want a sense of permanency in our relationships, in our activities, which means that we are seeking a lasting, continuous life in the stagnant pool; we don't want any real changes there, so we have built a society that guarantees us the permanency of property, of name, of fame.

But you see, life is not like that at all; life is not permanent. Like the leaves that fall from a tree, all things are impermanent, nothing endures; there is always change and death. Have you ever noticed a tree standing naked against the sky, how beautiful it is? All its branches are outlined, and in its nakedness there is a poem, there is a song. Every leaf is gone and it is waiting for the spring. When the spring comes it again fills the tree with the music of many leaves, which in due season fall and are blown away; and that is the way of life.

❖

THE FACT IS that life is like the river: endlessly moving on, ever seeking, exploring, pushing, overflowing its banks, penetrating every crevice with its water. But, you see, the mind won't allow that to happen to itself. The mind sees that it is dangerous, risky to live in a state of impermanency, insecurity, so it builds a wall around itself: the wall of tradition, of organized religion, of political and social theories. Family, name, property, the little virtues that we have cultivated—these are all within the walls, away from life. Life is moving, impermanent, and it ceaselessly tries to penetrate, to break down these walls, behind which there is confusion and misery. The gods within the walls are all false gods, and their writings and philosophies have no meaning because life is beyond them.

A MIND THAT is seeking permanency soon stagnates; like that pool along the river, it is soon full of corruption, decay. Only the mind that has no walls, no foothold, no barrier, no resting place, that is moving completely with life, timelessly pushing on, exploring, exploding—only such a mind can be happy, eternally new, because it is creative in itself.

Do you understand what I am talking about? You should, because all this is part of real education and, when you understand it, your whole life will be transformed, your relationship with the world, with your neighbour, with your wife or husband, will have a totally different meaning. Then you won't try to fulfil yourself through anything, seeing that the pursuit of fulfilment only invites sorrow and misery. That is why you should ask your teachers about all this and discuss it among yourselves. If you understand it, you will have begun to understand the extraordinary truth of what life is, and in that understanding there is great beauty and love, the flowering of goodness. But the efforts of a mind that is seeking a pool of security, of permanency, can only lead to darkness and corruption. Once established in the pool, such a mind is afraid to venture out, to seek, to explore; but truth, God, reality or what you will, lies beyond the pool.

Questioner: What is the work of man?

Krishnamurti: What do you think it is? Is it to study, pass examinations, get a job and do it for the rest of your life? Is it to go to the temple, join groups, launch various reforms? Is it man's work to kill animals for his own food? Is it man's work to build a bridge for the train to cross, to dig wells in a dry land, to find oil, to climb mountains, to conquer the earth and the air, to write poems, to paint, to love, to hate? Is all this the work of man? Building civilisations that come toppling down in a few centuries, bringing about wars, creating God in one's own image, killing people in the name of religion or the State, talking of peace and brotherhood while usurping power and being ruthless to others—this is what man is doing all around you, is it not? And is this the true work of man?

You can see that all this work leads to destruction and misery, to chaos and despair. Great luxuries exist side by side with extreme poverty; disease and starvation, with refrigerators and jet planes. All this is the work of man; and when you see it don't you ask yourself, 'Is that all? Is there not something else which is the true work of man?' If we can find out what is the true work of man, then jet planes, washing machines, bridges, houses will all have an entirely different meaning; but without finding out what is the true work of man, merely to indulge in reforms, in reshaping what man has already done, will lead nowhere.

So, what is the true work of man? Surely, the true work of man is to discover truth, God; it is to love and not to be caught in his own self-enclosing activities. In the very discovery of what is true there is love, and that love in man's relationship with man will create a different civilisation, a new world.

Bombay, 28 March 1948

Questioner: What are the foundations of right livelihood? How can I find out whether my livelihood is right, and how am I to find right livelihood in a basically wrong society?

Krishnamurti: In a basically wrong society, there cannot be right livelihood. What is happening throughout the world at the present time? Whatever livelihood we have brings us to war, to general misery and destruction, which is an obvious fact. Whatever we do inevitably leads to conflict, to decay, to ruthlessness and sorrow. So the present society is basically wrong; it is founded—is it not?—on envy, hate, and the desire for power, and such a society is bound to create wrong means of livelihood, such as the soldier, the policeman, and the lawyer. By their very nature, they are a disintegrating factor in society, and the more lawyers, policemen, and soldiers there are, the more obvious the decay of society. That is what is happening throughout the world: there are more soldiers, more policemen, more lawyers, and naturally the business man goes with them. All that has to be changed in order to found a right society—and we think such a task is impossible. It is not, but it is you and I who have to do it. Because at present whatever livelihood we undertake either creates misery for another, or leads to the ultimate destruction of mankind, which is shown in our daily existence. How can that be changed? It can be changed only when you and I are not seeking power, are not envious, are not full of hatred and antagonism. When you, in your relationship, bring about that transformation, then you are helping to create a new society, a society in which there are people who are not held by tradition, who do not ask anything for themselves, who are not pursuing power, because inwardly they are rich, they have found reality. Only the man who seeks reality can create a new society; only the man who loves can bring about a transformation in the world.

I know this is not a satisfactory answer for a person who wants to find out what is the right livelihood in the present structure of society. You must do the best you can in the present structure of society—either become a photographer, a merchant, a lawyer, a policeman, or whatever it is. But if you do, be conscious of what you are doing, be intelligent, be aware, fully cognizant, of what you are perpetuating, recognize the whole structure of society, with its corruption, with its hatred, with its envy; and if you yourself do not yield to these things, then perhaps you will be able to create a new society. But the moment you ask what is right livelihood, all these questions are inevitably there, are they not? You are not satisfied with your livelihood; you want to be envied, you want to have power, you want to have greater comforts and luxuries, position and authority, and therefore you are inevitably creating or maintaining a society that will bring destruction upon man, upon yourself.

If you clearly see that process of destruction in your own livelihood, if you see that it is the result of your own pursuit of livelihood, then obviously you will find the right means of earning money. But first you must see the picture of society as it is, a disintegrating, corrupted society; and when you see it very clearly, then your means of earning a livelihood will come. But first you must see the picture, see the world as it is, with its national divisions, with its cruelties, ambitions, hatreds, and controls. Then, as you see it more clearly, you will find that a right means of livelihood comes into being—you don't have to seek it. But the difficulty with most of us is that we have too many responsibilities; fathers, mothers are waiting for us to earn money and support them. And as it is difficult to get a job the way society is at the present time, any job is welcome; so we fall into the machinery of society. But those who are not so compelled, who have no need of an immediate job and can therefore look at the whole picture, it is they who are responsible. But you see, those who are not concerned with an immediate job are caught up in something else—they are concerned with their self-expansion, with their comforts, with their luxuries, with their amusements. They have time, but are dissipating it. And those who have time are responsible for the alteration of society; those who are not immediately pressed for a livelihood should really concern themselves with this whole problem of existence, and not get entangled in mere political action, in superficial activities. Those who have time and so-called leisure should seek out truth, because it is they who can bring about a revolution in the world, not the man whose stomach is empty. But, unfortunately, those who have leisure are not occupied with the eternal. They are occupied in filling their time. Therefore they also are a cause of misery and confusion in the world. So those of you who are listening, those of you who have a little time, should give thought and consideration to this problem, and by your own transformation you will bring about a world revolution.

Bangalore, 15 August 1948

Questioner: Can I remain a government official if I want to follow your teachings? The same question would arise with regard to so many professions. What is the right solution to the problem of livelihood?

Krishnamurti: Sirs, what do we mean by livelihood? It is the earning of one's needs—food, clothing, and shelter—is it not? The difficulty of livelihood arises only when we use the essentials of life, food, clothing, and shelter as means of psychological aggression. That is, when we use the needs, the necessities, as means of self-aggrandizement, then the problem of livelihood arises; our society is essentially based not on supplying the essentials, but on psychological aggrandizement, using the essentials as a psychological expansion of oneself. You have to think it out a little bit. Obviously, food, clothing, and shelter could be produced abundantly; there is enough scientific knowledge to supply the demand; but the demand for war is greater, not merely by the warmongers, but by each one of us, because each one of us is violent. There is sufficient scientific knowledge to give man all the necessities; it has been worked out, and they could be produced so that no man would be in need. Why does it not happen? Because no one is satisfied with food, clothing, and shelter. Each one wants something more, and, put in different words, the 'more' is power. But it would be brutish merely to be satisfied with needs. We will be satisfied with needs in the true sense, which is freedom from the desire for power, only when we have found the inner treasure that is imperishable, which you call God, truth, or what you will. If you can find those imperishable riches within yourself, then you are satisfied with few things, which few things can be supplied.

Unfortunately, we are carried away by sensate values. The values of the senses have become more important than the values of the real. After all, our whole social structure, our present civilisation, is essentially based on sensate values. Sensate values are not merely the values of the senses, but the values of thought, because thought is also the result of the senses; and when the mechanism of thought, which is the intellect, is cultivated, then there is in us a predominance of thought, which is also a sensory value. So as long as we are seeking sensate value, whether of touch, of taste, of smell, of perception, or of thought, the outer becomes far more significant than the inner; and the mere denial of the outer is not the way to the inner. You may deny the outer and withdraw from the world into a jungle or a cave and there think of God; but that very denial of the outer, that thinking of God, is still sensate because thought is sensate and any value based on the sensate is bound to create confusion—which is what is happening in the world at the present time. The sensate is dominant, and as long as the social structure is built on that, the means of livelihood becomes extraordinarily difficult.

So what is the right means of livelihood? This question can be answered only when there is a complete revolution in the present social structure, not according to the formula of the right or of the left, but a complete revolution in values that is not based on the sensate. Now, if those who have leisure—like the older people who are drawing their pensions, who have spent their earlier years seeking God or else various forms of destruction—really gave their time, their energy, to finding out the right solution, then they would act as a medium, as an instrument for bringing about revolution in the world. But they are not interested. They want security. They have worked so many years for their pensions, and they would like to live comfortably for the rest of their lives. They have time, but they are indifferent. They are only concerned with some abstraction that they call God, and that has no reference to the actual; but their abstraction is not God, it is a form of escape. And those who fill their lives with ceaseless activity are caught in the middle, they have not the time to find the answers to the various problems of life. So those who are concerned with these things, with bringing about a radical transformation in the world through the understanding of themselves, in them alone is there hope.

Surely we can see what is a wrong profession. To be a soldier, a policeman, a lawyer, is obviously a wrong profession, because they thrive on conflict, on dissension; and the big business man, the capitalist, thrives on exploitation. The big business man may be an individual, or it may be the State; if the State takes over big business it does not cease to exploit you and me. And as society is based on the army, the police, the law, the big business man, that is, on the principle of dissension, exploitation, and violence, how can you and I, who want a decent, right profession, survive? There is increasing unemployment, greater armies, larger police forces with their secret services, and big business is becoming bigger and bigger, forming vast corporations that are eventually taken over by the State—for the State has become a great corporation in certain countries. Given this situation of exploitation, of a society built on dissension, how are you going to find a right livelihood? It is almost impossible, is it not? Either you will have to go away and form a community with a few people—a self-supporting, co-operative community—or merely succumb to the vast machine. But you see, most of us are not interested in really finding the right livelihood. Most of us are concerned with getting a job and sticking to it in the hope of advancement with more and more pay. Because each one of us wants safety, security, a permanent position, there is no radical revolution. It is not those who are self-satisfied, contented, but only the adventurous, those who want to experiment with their lives, with their existence, who discover the real things, a new way of living.

So before there can be a right livelihood, the obviously false means of earning a livelihood must first be seen: the army, the law, the police, the big business corporations that are sucking people in and exploiting them, whether in the name of the State, of capital, or of religion. When you see the false and eradicate the false, there is transformation, there is revolution; and it is that revolution alone that can create a new society. To seek, as an individual, a right livelihood, is good, is excellent, but that does not solve the vast problem. The vast problem is solved only when you and I are not seeking security. There is no such thing as security. When you seek security, what happens? What is happening in the world at the present time? All Europe wants security, is crying for it, and what is happening? They want security through their nationalism. After all, you are a nationalist because you want security, and you think that through nationalism you are going to have security. It has been proved over and over again that you cannot have security through nationalism, because nationalism is a process of isolation, inviting wars, misery, and destruction. So right livelihood on a vast scale must begin with those who understand what is false. When you are battling against the false, then you are creating the right means of livelihood. When you are battling against the whole structure of dissension, of exploitation—whether by the left or by the right, or the authority of religion and the priests—that is the right profession at the present time; because that will create a new society, a new culture. But to battle, you must see very clearly and very definitely that which is false, so that the false drops away. To discover what is false, you must be aware of it, you must observe everything that you are doing, thinking, and feeling; and out of that you will not only discover what is false, but out of that there will come a new vitality, a new energy, and that energy will dictate what kind of work to do or not to do.

Poona, 17 October 1948

Questioner: While talking about right means of livelihood, you said that the profession of the army, of the lawyer, and of government service, were obviously not right means of livelihood. Are you not advocating withdrawal from society, and is that not running away from social conflicts and supporting the injustice and exploitation around us?

Krishnamurti: To transform anything or to understand anything you must first examine what is; then only is there a possibility of a renewal, a regeneration, a transformation. Merely to transform what is without understanding it, is a waste of time, a retrogression. Reform without understanding is retrogression, because we do not face what is. But if we begin to understand exactly what is, then we shall know how to act. You cannot act without first observing, discussing, and understanding what is. We must examine society as it is, with its weaknesses, its foibles, and to examine it we must see directly our connection, our relationship with it, not interposing an intellectual or theoretical explanation.

As society exists at present there is no choice between right livelihood and wrong livelihood. You take any you can get, if you are lucky enough to get one at all. So to the man who is pressed for an immediate job, there is no problem; he takes what he can get because he must eat. But to those of you who are not so immediately pressed, it should be a problem, and that is what we are discussing: What is the right means of livelihood in a society that is based on acquisition and class differences, on nationalism, greed, violence, and so on? Given these things, can there be right livelihood? Obviously not. And there are obviously wrong professions, wrong means of livelihood, such as the army, the lawyer, the police, and the government.

The army exists not for peace, but for war. It is the function of the army to create war, it is the function of the general to plan for war. If he does not, you will throw him out, won't you? You will get rid of him. The function of the general staff is to plan and prepare for future wars, and a general staff that does not plan for future wars is obviously inefficient. So the army is not a profession for peace, therefore it is not a right means of livelihood. I know the implications as well as you do. Armies will exist as long as sovereign governments exist with their nationalism and frontiers; and since you support sovereign governments you must support nationalism and war. Therefore, as long as you are a nationalist you have no choice about right livelihood.

Similarly, the police. The function of the police is to protect and to maintain things as they are. It also becomes the instrument of investigation, of inquisition, not only in the hands of totalitarian governments, but in the hands of any government. The function of the police is to snoop around, to investigate into the private lives of people. The more revolutionary you become, outwardly or inwardly, the more dangerous you are to government. That is why governments, and especially totalitarian governments, liquidate those who are outwardly or inwardly creating a revolution. So, obviously, the profession of police is not a right means of livelihood.

Similarly, the lawyer. He thrives on contention: It is essential for his livelihood that you and I should fight and wrangle. (Laughter.) You laugh it off. Probably many of you are lawyers, and your laugh indicates a mere nervous response to a fact; and through avoidance of that fact, you will still go on being lawyers. You may say that you are a victim of society, but you are victimized because you accept society as it is. So law is not a right means of livelihood. There can be right means of livelihood only when you do not accept the present state of things; and the moment you do not accept it, you do not accept law as a profession.

Similarly, you cannot expect to find right means of livelihood in the big corporations of business men who are amassing wealth, nor in the bureaucratic routine of government with its officials and red tape. Governments are only interested in maintaining things as they are, and if you become an engineer for the government you are directly or indirectly helping war.

As long as you accept society as it is, any profession, whether the army, the police, the law, or the government, is obviously not a right means of livelihood. Seeing that, what is an earnest man to do? Is he to run away and bury himself in some village? Even there he has to live somehow. He can beg, but the very food that is given to him comes indirectly from the lawyer, the policeman, the soldier, the government. And he cannot live in isolation, because that again is impossible; to live in isolation is to lie, both psychologically and physiologically. So what is one to do? All that one can do, if one is earnest, if one is intelligent about this whole process, is to reject the present state of things and give to society all that one is capable of. That is, sir, you accept food, clothing, and shelter from society, and you must give something to society in return. As long as you use the army, the police, the law, the government, as your means of livelihood, you maintain things as they are, you support dissension, inquisition, and war. But if you reject the things of society and accept only the essentials, you must give something in return. It is more important to find out what you are giving to society than to ask what is the right means of livelihood.

What are you giving to society? What is society? Society is relationship with one or with many. It is your relationship with another. What are you giving to another? Are you giving anything to another in the real sense of the word, or merely taking payment for something? As long as you do not find out what you are giving, whatever you take from society is bound to be a wrong means of livelihood. This is not a clever answer, and therefore you have to ponder, inquire into the whole question of your relationship to society. You may ask me in return, 'What are you giving to society in order that you be clothed, given shelter and food?' I am giving to society that of which I am talking today—which is not merely the verbal service any fool can give. I am giving to society what to me is true. You may reject it and say, 'Nonsense, it is not true.' But I am giving what to me is true, and I am far more concerned with that than with what society gives me. Sir, when you do not use society or your neighbour as a means of self-extension, you are completely content with the things that society gives you in the way of food, clothing, and shelter. Therefore you are not greedy; and not being greedy, your relationship with society is entirely different. The moment you do not use society as a means of self-extension, you reject the things of society, and therefore there is a revolution in your relationship. You are not depending on another for your psychological needs—and it is only then that you can have a right means of livelihood.

You may say this is all a very complicated answer, but it is not. Life has no simple answer. The man who looks for a simple answer to life has obviously a dull mind, a stupid mind. Life has no conclusion, life has no definite pattern; life is living, altering, changing. There is no positive, definite answer to life, but we can understand its whole significance and meaning. To understand, we must first see that we are using life as a means of self-extension, as a means of self-fulfilment; and because we are using life as a means of self-fulfilment, we create a society that is corrupt, that must begin to decay the very moment it comes into existence. So, an organized society has inherent in it the seed of decay.

It is very important for each one of us to find out what his relationship is with society, whether it is based on greed—which means self-extension, self-fulfilment, in which is implied power, position, authority—or if one merely accepts from society such essentials as food, clothing, and shelter. If your relationship is one of need and not of greed, then you will find the right means of livelihood wherever you are, even when society is corrupt. So, as the present society is disintegrating very rapidly, one has to find out; and those whose relationship is one of need only, will create a new culture, they will be the nucleus of society in which the necessities of life are equitably distributed and are not used as a means of self-extension. As long as society remains for you a means of self-extension, there must be a craving for power, and it is power that creates a society of classes divided as the high and the low, the rich and the poor, the man who has and the man who has not, the literate and the illiterate, each struggling with the other, all based on acquisitiveness and not on need. It is acquisitiveness that gives power, position, and prestige, and as long as that exists, your relationship with society must be a wrong means of livelihood. There can be right means of livelihood when you look to society only for your needs—and then your relationship with society is very simple. Simplicity is not the 'more', nor is it the putting on of a loin cloth and renouncing the world. Merely limiting yourself to a few things is not simplicity. Simplicity of the mind is essential, and that simplicity of the mind cannot exist if the mind is used for self-extension, self-fulfilment, whether that self-fulfilment comes through the pursuit of God, of knowledge, of money, property, or position. The mind that is seeking God is not a simple mind, for its God is its own projection. The simple man is he who sees exactly what is and understands it—he does not demand anything more. Such a mind is content, it understands what is—which does not mean accepting society as it is, with its exploitation, classes, wars, and so on. But a mind that sees and understands what is, and therefore acts, such a mind has few needs, it is very simple, quiet. And it is only when the mind is quiet that it can receive the eternal.

Bombay, 26 February 1950

Questioner: The more one listens to you, the more one feels that you are preaching withdrawal from life. I am a clerk in the Secretariat. I have four children, and I get only 125 rupees a month. Will you please explain how I can fight the gloomy struggle for existence in the new way you are proposing? Do you really think that your message can mean anything significant to the starving and the stunted wage-earner? Have you lived among such people?

Krishnamurti: First of all, let us dispose of the question as to whether I have lived among such people. It implies—does it not?—that in order to understand life you must go through every phase of life, every experience, you must live among the poor and the rich, you must starve and pass through every condition of existence. Now, to put the problem very briefly, must you go through drunkenness to know sobriety? Does not one experience fully, completely understood, reveal the whole process of life? Must you go through all the phases of life to understand life? Please see that this is not an avoidance of the question—on the contrary. We think that to know wisdom we must go through every phase of life and experience, from the rich man to the poor man, from the beggar to the king. Is that so? Is wisdom the accumulation of many experiences? Or is wisdom to be found in the complete understanding of one experience? Because we never completely and fully understand one experience, we wander from experience to experience, hoping for some salvation, for some refuge, for some happiness. We have made our life a process of continuous accumulation of experiences, and therefore it is an endless struggle, a ceaseless battle to attain, to acquire. Surely that is a tedious, an utterly stupid approach to life, is it not?

Is it not possible to gather the full significance of an experience and so understand the whole width and depth of life? I say it is possible, and that it is the only way to understand life. Whatever the experience, whatever the challenge and response to life, if one can understand it fully, then the pursuit of every experience has no meaning, it becomes merely a waste of time. Because we are incapable of doing that, we have invented the illusory idea that by accumulating experiences we shall ultimately arrive—God knows where!

The questioner wants to know if I am preaching withdrawal from life. What do we mean by life? I am thinking out this problem aloud, so let us follow it together. What do we mean by life? Living is possible only in relationship, is it not? If there is no relationship, there is no life. To be is to be related; life is a process of relationship, of being in communion with another—with two or ten—with society. Life is not a process of isolation, of withdrawal. But for most of us, living is a process of isolation, is it not? We are struggling to isolate ourselves in action, in relationship. All our activities are self-enclosing, narrowing down, isolating, and in that very process there is friction, sorrow, pain. Living is relationship, and nothing can exist in isolation; therefore there can be no withdrawal from life. On the contrary, there must be the understanding of relationship—your relationship with your wife, your children, with society, with nature, with the beauty of this day, the sunlight on the waters, the flight of a bird, with the things that you possess and the ideals that control you. To understand all that, you do not withdraw from it. Truth is not found in withdrawal and isolation; on the contrary, in isolation, whether it is conscious or unconscious, there is only darkness and death.

So I am not proposing a withdrawal from life, a suppression of life. On the contrary, we can understand life only in relationship. It is because we do not understand life that we are all the time making an effort to withdraw, to isolate, and having created a society based on violence, on corruption, God becomes the ultimate isolation.

Then the questioner wants to know how, earning so little, he is to live what we are talking about. Now, first of all, the earning of a livelihood is not only the problem of the man who earns little, but it is also yours and mine, is it not? You may have a little more money, you may be well off, have a better job, a better position, a bigger bank account; but it is also your problem and mine, because this society is what all of us have created. Until we three—you, I, and another—really understand relationship, we cannot bring about revolution in society. The man who has no food in his stomach obviously cannot find reality, he must first be fed. But the man whose stomach is full, surely it is his immediate responsibility to see that there is a fundamental revolution in society, that things do not go on as they are. To think, to feel out all these problems is much more the responsibility of those who have time, who have leisure, than it is of the man who earns little and has such a struggle to make both ends meet, who has no time and is worn out by this rotten, exploiting society. It is you and I, those of us who have a little more time and leisure, who must go into these problems completely—which does not mean that we have to become professional talkers, offering one system as a substitute for another. It is for you and I who have time, who have leisure for thought, to seek out the way of a new society, a new culture.

Now what happens to the poor man who is earning 125 rupees? He has to carry the family with him, he has to accept the superstitions of his grandmother, his aunts, nephews, and so on; he has to marry according to a certain pattern, he has to do rituals, ceremonies, and fit in with all that superstitious nonsense. He is caught in it, and if he rebels, you, the respectable people, throttle him.

So the question of right livelihood is your problem and mine, is it not? But most of us are not concerned with right livelihood at all. We are glad and thankful simply to have a job, and so we maintain a society, a culture, that renders right livelihood impossible. Sirs, do not treat it theoretically. If you find yourself in a wrong vocation and actually do something about it, do you not see what a revolution it will bring in your life and in the life of those around you? But if you listen casually and carry on as before because you have a good job and for you there is no problem, obviously you will continue to cause misery in the world. For the man with too little money there is a problem, but he, like the rest of us, is only concerned with having more. And when he gets more the problem continues, because he wants still more.

What is a right means of livelihood? Obviously, there are certain occupations that are detrimental to society. The army is detrimental to society because it plans and encourages murder in the name of the country. Because you are nationalists, holding to sovereign governments, you must have armed forces to protect your property; and property is much more important to you than life, the life of your sons. That is why you have conscription, that is why your schools are being encouraged to have military training. In the name of your country you are destroying your children. Your country is yourself identified, your own projection, and when you worship your country you are sacrificing your children to the worship of yourself. That is why the army, which is the instrument of a separate and sovereign government, is a wrong means of livelihood. But it is made easy to enter the army, and it becomes a sure means of earning a little money. Just see this extraordinary fact in modern civilisation. Surely the army is a wrong way to earn one's livelihood, because it is based on planned and calculated destruction. Until you and I see the truth of this we are not going to bring about any different kind of society.

Similarly, you can see that a job in a police force is a wrong means of livelihood. Do not smile and pass it off. The police becomes a means of investigating private lives. We are not talking of the police as a means of helping, guiding, but as an instrument of the state, the secret police, and all the rest of it. Then the individual becomes merely an instrument of society, the individual has no privacy, no freedom, no rights of his own; he is investigated, controlled, shaped by the government, which is society. Obviously, that is a wrong means of livelihood.

Then there is the profession of law. Is that not a wrong means of livelihood? I see some of you are smiling. Probably you are lawyers, and you know better than I do what that system is based on. Fundamentally, not superficially, it is based on maintaining things as they are, on disagreements, disputation, confusion, quarrels, encouraging disruption and disorder in the name of order.

There is also the wrong profession of the man who wants to become rich, the big business man, the man who is gathering, accumulating, storing up money through exploitation, through ruthlessness—though he may do it in the name of philanthropy or in the name of education.

Obviously, then, these are all wrong means of livelihood, and a complete change in the social structure, a revolution of the right kind, is possible only when it begins with you. Revolution cannot be based on an ideal or a system; but when you see all this as a fact, you are liberated from it, and therefore you are free to act. But, sirs, you do not want to act. You are afraid of being disturbed, and you say, 'There is already sufficient confusion, please do not make any more.' If you do not make more confusion, others are there making it for you—and utilizing that confusion as a means of gaining political power. Surely it is your responsibility as an individual to see the confusion within and without, and to do something about it—not merely accept it and wait for a miracle, a marvellous Utopia created by others into which you can step without effort.

Sirs, this problem is your problem as well as the poor man's problem. The poor man depends on you and you depend on him; he is your clerk while you ride in a big car and get a fat salary, accumulating money at his expense. So it is your problem as well as his, and until you and he alter radically in your relationship, there will be no real revolution; though there may be violence and bloodshed, you will maintain things essentially as they are. Therefore our problem is the transformation of relationship; and that transformation is not on the intellectual or verbal level, but it can take place only when you understand the fact of what you are. You cannot understand it if you theorize, verbalize, deny, or justify, and that is why it is important to understand the whole process of the mind. A revolution that is merely the outcome of the mind is no revolution at all, but revolution that is not of the mind, that is not of the word, of the system is the only revolution, the only solution to the problem. But unfortunately, we have cultivated our brains, our so-called intellects, to such an extent that we have lost all capacities except the merely intellectual and verbal capacity. It is only when we see life as a whole, in its entirety, in its totality, that there is a possibility of a revolution that will give both the poor man and the rich man his due.

From The Urgency of Change

Beauty and the Artist

Questioner: I wonder what an artist is? There on the banks of the Ganges, in a dark little room, a man sits weaving a most beautiful sari in silk and gold, and in Paris in his atelier another man is painting a picture that he hopes will bring him fame. Somewhere there is a writer cunningly spinning out stories stating the old, old problem of man and woman; then there is the scientist in his laboratory and the technician putting together a million parts so that a rocket may go to the moon. And in India a musician is living a life of great austerity in order to transmit faithfully the distilled beauty of his music. There is the housewife preparing a meal, and the poet walking alone in the woods. Aren't these all artists in their own way? I feel that beauty is in the hands of everybody, but they don't know it. The man who makes beautiful clothes or excellent shoes, the woman who arranged those flowers on your table, all of them seem to work with beauty. I often wonder why it is that the painter, the sculptor, the composer, the writer—the so-called creative artists—have such extraordinary importance in this world and not the shoemaker or the cook. Aren't they creative too? When you consider all the varieties of expression that people consider beautiful, then what place has a true artist in life, and who is the true artist? It is said that beauty is the very essence of all life. Is that building over there, which is considered to be so beautiful, the expression of that essence? I should greatly appreciate it if you would go into this whole question of beauty and the artist.

Krishnamurti: Surely the artist is one who is skilled in action? This action is in life and not outside of life. Therefore, if it is living skilfully that truly makes an artist, this skill can operate for a few hours in the day when he is playing an instrument, writing poems, or painting pictures, or it can operate a bit more if he is skilled in many such fragments—like those great men of the Renaissance who worked in several different media. But the few hours of music or writing may contradict the rest of his living, which is in disorder and confusion. So is such a man an artist at all? The man who plays the violin with artistry and keeps his eye on his fame isn't interested in the violin, he is only exploiting it to be famous, the 'me' is far more important than the music, and so it is with the writer or the painter with an eye on fame. The musician identifies his 'me' with what he considers to be beautiful music, and the religious man identifies his 'me' with what he considers to be the sublime. All these are skilled in their particular little fields but the rest of the vast field of life is disregarded. So we have to find out what is skill in action, in living, not only in painting or in writing or in technology, but how one can live the whole of life with skill and beauty. Are skill and beauty the same? Can a human being—whether he be an artist or not—live the whole of his life with skill and beauty? Living is action and when that action breeds sorrow it ceases to be skilful. So can a man live without sorrow, without friction, without jealousy and greed, without conflict of any kind? The issue is not who is an artist and who is not an artist but whether a human being, you or another, can live without torture and distortion. Of course it is profane to belittle great music, great sculpture, great poetry or dancing, or to sneer at it; that is to be unskilled in one's own life. But the artistry and beauty that is skill in action should operate throughout the day, not just during a few hours of the day. This is the real challenge, not just playing the piano beautifully. You must play it beautifully if you touch it at all, but that is not enough. It is like cultivating a small corner of a huge field. We are concerned with the whole field and that field is life. What we always do is to neglect the whole field and concentrate on fragments, our own or other people's. Artistry is to be completely awake and therefore to be skilful in action in the whole of life. And this is beauty.

Q: What about the factory worker or the office employee? Is he an artist? Doesn't his work preclude skill in action, and so deaden him that he has no skill in anything else either? Is he not conditioned by his work?

K: Of course he is. But if he wakes up he will either leave his work or so transform it that it becomes artistry. What is important is not the work but the waking up to the work. What is important is not the conditioning of the work but to wake up.

Q: What do you mean, wake up?

K: Are you awakened only by circumstances, by challenges, by some disaster or joy? Or is there a state of being awake without any cause? If you are awakened by an event, a cause, then you depend on it, and when you depend on something—whether it be a drug, sex, painting, or music—you are allowing yourself to be put to sleep. So any dependence is the end of skill, the end of artistry.

Q: What is this other awakened state that has no cause? You are talking about a state in which there is neither a cause nor an effect. Can there be a state of mind that is not the result of some cause? I don't understand that, because surely everything we think and everything we are is the result of a cause. There is the endless chain of cause and effect.

K: This chain of cause and effect is endless because the effect becomes the cause and the cause begets further effects, and so on.

Q: Then what action is there outside this chain?

K: All we know is action with a cause, a motive, action which is a result. All action is in relationship. If relationship is based on cause it is cunning adaptation, and therefore inevitably leads to another form of dullness. Love is the only thing that is causeless, that is free; it is beauty, it is skill, it is art. Without love there is no art. When the artist is playing beautifully there is no 'me'; there is love and beauty, and this is art. This is skill in action. Skill in action is the absence of the 'me'. Art is the absence of the 'me'. But when you neglect the whole field of life and concentrate only on a little part—however much the 'me' may then be absent, you are still living unskilfully and therefore you are not an artist of life. The absence of 'me' in living is love and beauty, which brings its own skill. This is the greatest art: living skilfully in the whole field of life.

Q: Oh Lord! How am I to do that? I see it and feel it in my heart, but how can I maintain it?

K: There is no way to maintain it, there is no way to nourish it, there is no practising of it; there is only the seeing of it. Seeing is the greatest of all skills.

Bombay, 11 March 1953

I THINK IT might be worthwhile if we went into the question of how quickly the mind deteriorates and what are the primary factors that make the mind dull, insensitive, quick to respond. I think it would be significant if we could go into this question why the mind deteriorates, because perhaps in understanding that, we may be able to find out what is really a simple life.

We notice as we grow older that the mind, the instrument of understanding, the instrument with which we probe into any problem, to inquire, to question, to discover—that mind if misused, deteriorates, disintegrates; and it seems to me that one of the major factors of this deterioration of the mind is the process of choice.

All our life is based on choice. We choose at different levels of our existence. We choose between white and blue, between one flower and another flower, between certain psychological impulses of like and dislike, between certain ideas, beliefs, accepting some and discarding others. So our mental structure is based on this process of choice, this continuous effort of choosing, distinguishing, discarding, accepting, rejecting. And in that process there is constant struggle, constant effort. There is never a direct comprehension, but always the tedious process of accumulation of the capacity to distinguish—which is really based on memory, on the accumulation of knowledge—and therefore there is this constant effort made through choice.

Now, is not choice ambition? Our life is ambition. We want to be somebody, we want to be well thought of, want to achieve a result. If I am not wise, I want to become wise. If I am violent, I want to become non-violent. The becoming is the process of ambition. Whether I want to become the biggest politician or the most perfect saint, the ambition, the drive, the impulse of becoming is the process of choice, is the process of ambition, which is essentially based on choice.

So our life is a series of struggles, a movement from one ideological concept, formula, desire, to another, and in this process of becoming, in this process of struggle the mind deteriorates. The very nature of this deterioration is choice; and we think choice is necessary, choice from which springs ambition.

Now can we find a way of life that is not based on ambition, that is not of choice, that is a flowering in which the result is not sought? All that we know of life is a series of struggles ending in result, and those results are being discarded for greater results. That is all we know.

In the case of the man who sits alone in a cave, in the very process of making himself perfect there is choice, and that choice is ambition. The man who is violent tries to become non-violent; that very becoming is ambition. We are not trying to find out whether ambition is right or wrong, whether it is essential to life, but whether it is conducive to a life of simplicity. I do not mean the simplicity of a few clothes, that is not a simple life. The putting on of a loin cloth does not indicate a man that is simple; on the contrary, it may be that, by the renunciation of the outer things, the mind becomes more ambitious for it tries to hold on to its own ideal that it has projected and that it has created.

So if we observe our own ways of thinking, should we not inquire into this question of ambition? What do we mean by it, and is it possible to live without ambition? We see that ambition breeds competition, whether in children in school, or among the big politicians, all the way up—trying to beat a record. This ambition produces certain industrial benefits, but in its wake, obviously, there is the darkening of the mind, the technological conditioning, so that the mind loses its pliability, its simplicity and therefore is incapable of directly experiencing. Should we not inquire, not as a group but as individuals—you and I—should we not find out what this ambition means, whether we are at all aware of this ambition in our life?

When we offer ourselves to serve the country, to do noble work, is there not in it the fundamental element of ambition, which is the way of choice? And is not therefore choice a corruptive influence in our life, because it prevents the flowering? The man who flowers is the man who is, who is not becoming.

Is there not a difference between the flowering mind and the becoming mind? The becoming mind is a mind that is always growing, becoming, enlarging, gathering experience as knowledge. We know that process full well in our daily life, with all its results, with all its conflicts, its miseries and strife, but we do not know the life of flowering. And is there not a difference between the two that we have to discover—not by trying to demarcate, to separate—but to discover in the process of our living? When we discover this, we may perhaps be able to set aside this ambition, the way of choice, and discover a flowering, which is the way of life, which may be true action.

So if we merely say that we must not be ambitious without the discovery of the flowering way of life, the mere killing of ambition destroys the mind also, because it is an action of the will that is the action of choice. So is it not essential for each one of us to find out in our lives the truth of ambition? We are all encouraged to be ambitious, our society is based on it, the strength of the drive towards a result. And in that ambition there are inequalities that legislation tries to level out, to alter. Perhaps that way, that approach to life is essentially wrong, and there might be another approach that is the flowering of life, that could express itself without accumulation. After all, we know when we are conscious of striving after something, of becoming something; that is ambition, the seeking of a result.

But there is an energy, a force in which there is a compulsion without the process of accumulation, without the background of the 'me', of the self, of the ego. That is the way of creativity.

Without understanding that, without actually experiencing that, our life becomes very dull, our life becomes a series of endless conflicts in which there is no creativity, no happiness. And perhaps if we can understand—not by discarding ambition but by understanding the ways of ambition—by being open, by comprehending, by listening to the truth of ambition, perhaps we may come upon that creativity in which there is a continuous expression that is not the expression of self-fulfilment but is the expression of energy without the limitation of the 'me'.

Questioner: Will you please tell us what you mean by the words *our vocation*? I gather you mean something different from the ordinary connotation of these words.

Krishnamurti: Each one of us pursues some kind of vocation—the lawyer, the soldier, the policeman, the business man, and so on. Obviously there are certain vocations that are detrimental to society—the lawyer, the soldier, the policeman, and the industrialist who is not making other men equally rich.

When we want, when we choose a particular vocation, when we train our children to follow a particular vocation, are we not creating a conflict within society? You choose one vocation and I choose another. Does that not bring about conflict between us? Is that not what is happening in the world, because we have never found out what is our true vocation? We are only being conditioned by society, by a particular culture, to accept certain forms of vocations that breed competition and hatred between man and man. We know that, we see it.

Now is there any other way of living in which you and I can function in our true vocations? Is there not one vocation for man? Please listen, sirs. Are there different vocations for man? We see that there are: you are a clerk, I polish shoes; you are an engineer and I am a politician. We see innumerable varieties of vocations and we see they are all in conflict with each other. So man through his vocation is in conflict, in hatred, with man. We know that. With that we are familiar every day.

Now let us find out if there is not one vocation for man. If we can all find it, then the expression of different capacities will not bring about conflict between man and man. I say there is only one vocation for man. There is only one vocation, not many. The one vocation for man is to find out what is real. Sirs, don't settle back. This is not a mystical answer.

If I and you are finding out what is truth, which is our true vocation, then in the search of that we will not be in competition. I shall not be competing with you, I shall not fight you though you may express that truth in a different way. You may be the Prime Minister, I shall not be ambitious and want to occupy your place, because I am seeking equally with you what is truth. Therefore, as long as we do not find out that true vocation of man, we must be in competition with each other, we must hate each other. And whatever legislation you may pass, on that level you can only produce further chaos.

Is it not possible from childhood, through right education, through the right educator, to help the boy, the student, to be free to find out what is the truth about everything—not just truth in the abstract, but to find out the truth of all relationships—the boy's relationship to machinery, his relationship to nature, his relationship to money, to society, to government, and so on? That requires—does it not?—a different kind of teachers who are concerned with helping or giving the boy, the student, freedom so that he begins to investigate the cultivation of intelligence, which can never be conditioned by a society that is always deteriorating.

So is there not one vocation for man? Man cannot exist in isolation. He exists only in relationship, and when in that relationship there is no discovery of truth, the discovery of the truth of relationship, then there is conflict.

There is only one vocation for you and me. And in the search of that, we shall find the expression wherein we shall not come into conflict, we shall not destroy each other. But it must begin surely through right education, through the right educator. The educator also needs education. Fundamentally the teacher is not merely the giver of information, but brings about in the student, the freedom, the revolt to discover what is truth.

From a Talk with Students at Rajghat School, 20 January 1954

ONE OF THE greatest difficulties that we have is to find out what makes for mediocrity. You know what that word means? A mediocre mind really means a mind that is impaired, that is not free, that is caught in fear, in a problem; a mind that merely revolves round its own self-interest, round its own success and failure about its own immediate solutions and the sorrows that inevitably come to a petty mind. It is one of the most difficult things—is it not?—for a mind that is mediocre to break away from its own habits of thought, from its own pattern of action, and be free to live, to be able to move about, to act. You will see most of our minds are very small, are very petty. Look at your own mind and you will see what it is occupied with—such small things as your passing an examination, what people will think of you, how you are afraid of somebody, and your own success. You want a job, and when you have that job you want to have a better job and so on. If you search your mind you will find it is all the time occupied with this kind of small, trivial self-interested activities. Being thus occupied, it creates problems, doesn't it? It tries to solve its problems according to its own pettiness and, not doing that, it increases its own problems. It seems to me that the function of education is to break down this way of thinking.

The mediocre mind, the mind that is caught in one of the narrow streets of Varanasi and lives there, may read, it may pass examinations, it may be socially very active, but it still lives in the narrow little street of its own making. I think it is very important for all of us—the old and the young—to see that the mind being so small, whatever effort it makes, whatever struggles it may go through, whatever hopes or fears or longings it may have, is still small, is still petty. It is very difficult for most of us to realize that the gurus, the Masters, the societies, the religions that the petty mind forms, are still petty. It is very difficult to break this pattern of thinking.

Is it not very important while we are young to have teachers, educators who are not mediocre? Because if the educators are dull, weary, are thinking of little things and are caught in their own pettiness, naturally they cannot help to bring about an atmosphere in which the student can be free and break through the pattern that society has imposed upon people.

I think it is very important to be able to know that one is mediocre, because most of us do not admit we are mediocre, we all think that we have something extraordinary lurking behind somewhere. But we have to know that we are mediocre, to realize that mediocrity still creates pettiness, and not to act against it. Any action against mediocrity is the action born of mediocrity; to break down mediocrity is still petty, trivial. Do you understand all this? Unfortunately, I speak only in English, but I wish your teachers could help you to understand this. In explaining this to you, their own triviality will break down. The mere explanation will awaken them to their own pettiness, smallness. That is why a small mind cannot love, is not generous, quarrels over trivial things. What is needed in India and elsewhere in the world is not clever people, not people with degrees or big positions, but people like you and me who have broken down the triviality of their minds.

Triviality is essentially the thought of oneself. That is what makes the mind trivial, the constant occupation about its own success, about its own ideals, about its own desires to become perfect. That is what makes the mind petty because the 'me', the self, however much it may expand, is still very small. So the mind that is occupied is a petty mind; the mind that is constantly thinking about something, worried about its own examination, worried as to whether it will get a job, what the father and mother or teachers or gurus or neighbours or society thinks, is a petty mind. The occupation with these ideas makes for respectability, and the respectable mind, the mediocre mind, is not a happy mind. Please listen to all this.

You know you all want to be respectable—don't you?—to be well thought of by somebody—by your father or by your neighbour or by your society—to do the right thing, and this creates fear. Such a mind can never think of anything new. What is needed in this deteriorated world is a mind that is creative, not inventing, not just having capacity. But that creativeness comes when there is no fear, when the mind is not occupied with its own problems. All this requires an atmosphere in which the student is really free, free not to do whatever he likes but free to question, to investigate, to find out, to reason and to go beyond the reason. The student requires a freedom in which he can find out what he really loves to do in life so that he is not forced to do a particular thing that he loathes, that he does not like.

You know that a mediocre mind never revolts; it submits to government, to parental authority; it puts up with anything. I am afraid in a country like this, where there is overpopulation, where livelihood is very very difficult, the pressures of these make us obey, make us submit, and gradually the spirit of revolt, the spirit of discontent is destroyed. A school of this kind should educate a student to have that tremendous discontent right through life, not easily to be satisfied. The discontent begins to find out, becomes really intelligent, if it does not find a channel of satisfaction, of gratification.

Questioner: Is it right that fame comes after death?

Krishnamurti: Do you think that the villager who dies will have fame after he dies?

Q: A great man, after he dies, becomes famous and is honoured.

K: What is a great man? Find out the truth of that question. Is he one who seeks fame? Is he one who would give himself tremendous importance? Is he one who identifies himself with a country and becomes the leader? If he does this, he has fame while he is living. That is all that we want. We all want the same thing; we all want to be great people. You want to lead the procession, you want to be the governor, you want to be the great ideal, the great person who is going to reform India. Since you want that, since all the people want that, you will lead the procession. But is that greatness? Does greatness consist in being publicized, in having your name appear in the papers, having authority over people, making people obey because you have a strong will or personality or crook in the mind? Surely, greatness is something totally different.

Greatness is anonymity. To be anonymous is the greatest thing. The great cathedral, the great things of life, great sculpture, must be anonymous. They do not belong to any particular person. Like truth; truth does not belong to you or to me, it is totally impersonal and anonymous. If you say you have got truth, when you say you have got truth, then you are not anonymous, you are far more important than truth. But an anonymous person may never be great. Probably he will never be great, because he does not want to be great, great in the sense of the world, or even inwardly. Because he is nobody. He has no followers. He has no shrine, he does not puff himself up. But most of us unfortunately want to puff ourselves up, we want to be great, we want to be known, we want to have success. Success leads to fame, but that is an empty thing, is it not? It is like ashes. Every politician is known and it is his business to be known and therefore he is not great. Greatness is to be unknown, inwardly and outwardly to be as nothing; and that requires great penetration, great understanding, great affection.

Amsterdam, 23 May 1955

Questioner: A man fully occupied is kept busy day and night in his own subconsciousness with practical problems that have to be solved. Your vision can only be realized in the stillness of self-awareness. There is hardly any time for stillness; the immediate is too urgent. Can you give any practical suggestion?

Krishnamurti: Sir, what do we mean by 'practical suggestion'? Something that you should do immediately? Some system that you should practise in order to produce a stillness of the mind? After all, if you practise a system, that system will produce a result; but it will only be the result of the system, and not your own discovery, not that which you find in being aware of yourself in your contacts in daily life. A system obviously produces its own result. However much you may practise it, for whatever length of time, the result will always be dictated by the system, the method. It will not be a discovery, it will be a thing imposed on the mind through its desire to find a way out of this chaotic, sorrowful world.

So what is one to do when one is so busy, occupied night and day—as most people are—with earning a livelihood? First of all, is one occupied the whole of the time with business, with a livelihood? Or does one have periods during the day when you are not so occupied? I think those periods when you are not so occupied are far more important than the periods in which you are occupied.

Isn't it very important to find out what the mind is occupied with? If it is occupied, consciously occupied, with business affairs all the time—which is really impossible—then there is obviously no space, no quietness, in which to find anything new. Fortunately, most of us are not occupied entirely with our business, and there are moments when we can probe into ourselves, be aware. I think those periods are far more significant than our periods of occupation, and if we allow it those moments will begin to shape, to control, our business activities, our daily life.

After all, the conscious mind, the mind that is so occupied, obviously has no time for any deeper thought. But the conscious mind is not the whole entirety of the mind; there is also the unconscious part. Can the conscious mind delve into the unconscious? That is, can the conscious mind, the mind that wants to inquire, to analyze, can that probe into the unconscious? Or must the conscious mind be still in order for the unconscious to give its hints, its intimations? Is the unconscious so very different from the conscious, or is the totality of the mind the conscious as well as the unconscious? The totality of the mind, as we know it—conscious and unconscious—is educated, is conditioned, with all the various impositions of culture, tradition, and memory. And perhaps the answer to all our problems is not within the field of the mind at all; it may be outside it. To find that which is the true answer to all the complex problems of our existence, of our daily struggle, surely the mind, the conscious as well as the unconscious, must be totally still, must it not?

And the questioner wants to know, when he is so busy, what shall he do? Surely he is not so busy; surely he does amuse himself occasionally. If he begins to give some time during the day, five minutes, ten minutes, half an hour, in order to reflect upon these matters, then that very reflection brings longer periods in which he will have time to think, to delve. So I do not think mere superficial occupation of the mind has much significance. There is something far more important, which is to find out the operation of the mind, the ways of our own thinking, the motives, the urges, the memories, the traditions, in which the mind is caught. And we can do that while we are earning our livelihood, so that we become fully conscious of ourselves and our peculiarities. Then I think it is possible for the mind to be really quiet, and so to find that which is beyond its own projections.

From a Dialogue with Young People at Saanen, 5 August 1972

Krishnamurti: How does youth respond to the modern challenge? The challenge being not merely social reform, not merely a political revolution with a different kind of politics, honesty, more or less incorruptibility. There are vast changes taking place technologically and physiologically. There is a breaking up of religions, and it's a tremendous challenge. How does youth respond to it? Is that a fair question? You are supposed to be young, how do you respond to it? Respond to the total challenge, not just form a little commune, or take to drugs, or say, 'Well, the old people don't understand young people.' There is the generation gap. But there is this enormous challenge. How do you young people respond to it?

K: Earning a livelihood is a problem that is not psychological. You have to live in this world, you can't run away from it.

Questioner: I would like to ask whether it is possible to act completely without being fragmentary, and to go into the question of whether it's possible to go into a school, an establishment type of public school where it is like a gigantic machine, a programme, and somehow actually do something?

K: The question is: I am a teacher in a school that is mechanical, that is overcrowded, all the rest of it; how am I to act there totally, without being crushed by this vast structure? If I have to teach fifty or sixty boys in a class and the boys are rowdy and all the rest of it, how am I to deal with that? How am I to act totally in those given circumstances. What am I to do? I must answer this question, please. I earn my livelihood at teaching in a school, in a system, that is over-burdened. How am I, given this condition, to teach wholly? Can you do it?

Q: Let's say that I've not so far succeeded, in fact I've been fired.

K: Quite right, sir. You can't do it. It can't be done. Look, teaching fifty boys in a class, where you want to teach them, say, mathematics, and you're not merely concerned with teaching mathematics, you're concerned with their minds, bringing about their intelligence, making them behave properly, the whole of it—with fifty boys you can't do it. Therefore you're fired; what will you do? Just go into another profession? Or say, 'By Jove, teaching is the most important thing, because that deals with young people, creating new minds'—all the rest of it—'tremendously important. I'll find out with others, with the few who feel this thing, and start a school.' This means *tremendous* energy, which means you are giving your whole life for it, not just casual action.

K: Now, we'll answer the person who says, 'I live in a city and I have to earn a livelihood there; I have no time, therefore I'll withdraw and form a little commune.'

I go away with a few friends if I can, and we live together cultivating our own garden . . . and have time to think how to bring about this total action. Is it my intention when I go and live with a few people—is it my true, real intention—to find out a way of life in which there is total action?. . . I go away from the present structure of society and try to live a life in which I comprehend this total movement of existence. The monks have tried to do it, various communes have tried to do this; they either accept the authority of a person, or the authority of a belief, or the authority of the necessity of working together. Or does one go, discarding *all* authority of persons, or the necessity that we must live together in order to give time to think? Do you discard that and therefore find out for yourself what is the way of existence, of living that will not be fragmentary, that will act economically, psychologically, and more, in a whole manner? So it depends on you, on what your serious intention is, whether inwardly as well as outwardly you want to live differently.

Q: Sir, are you saying that the making of a commune or going to business are the same thing? It is no action at all, but realizing that, this is action.

K: Yes, sir. You do it; you do it on a practical level, but that practical level depends on your intention, on the depth of your honesty.

Q: Does all intentional behaviour have some ideal behind it?

K: That's just it. How do you respond to all this? Run off to a church, join a political activity, become a Communist, this or that, or lead a completely irresponsible life because your father, some friends will give you money, therefore you don't care?. . .

Q: What you have to do all the time is to live on the practical level; you sleep in the barns or you sleep in a hotel, or try to do something. But if you don't have money. . .

K: I met a young boy in India. He made his way across the continent, hitch-hiking from California to New York, took work as a sailor, came by boat to India, worked there, and I met him on the seashore. To him what was important was to find out what truth was. You may say, how silly that is, but he wanted to find out. Therefore he gave his life to it, he didn't talk about practical life, he worked. If you have money, or if your parents have money or friends give you money, then you have the problem of depending on somebody, your parents, but you can play around with all these ideas.

So we come to the point again: Are you aware that any kind of fragmentary action is really the most unintelligent, mischievous action? That's what the old establishment has done. That's their way of life: keep the business world in one way, religion for Sunday, and politics on Thursday. You know, all the rest of it! And you are doing exactly the same thing only calling it by a different name. And I say you, as the young who are supposed to be vigorous, enthusiastic, to have tremendous vitality to act, knowing what the older generation have done, are as confused as the others. Therefore there is no generation gap at all. Do you see that makes us realize how hypocritical we are? You deny the old establishment and you are doing exactly the same thing as they do, only in other words. So as you are young, you have to create a new world. You are responsible for a new world. And if you say, 'Well, I'm only concerned with money or only with psychological things', it has no meaning.

From Krishnamurti on Education, *Chapter 8*

Talk with Students: On Image Making

WHEN WE ARE very young it is a delight to be alive, to hear the birds of the morning, to see the hills after rain, to see those rocks shining in the sun, the leaves sparkling, to see the clouds go by and to rejoice on a clear morning with a full heart and a clear mind. We lose this feeling when we grow up, with worries, anxieties, quarrels, hatreds, fears, and the everlasting struggle to earn a livelihood. We spend our days in battle with each other, disliking and liking, with a little pleasure now and then. We never hear the birds, see the trees as we once saw them, see the dew on the grass and the bird on the wing and the shiny rock on a mountainside glistening in the morning light. We never see all that when we are grown up. Why? I do not know if you have ever asked that question. I think it necessary to ask it. If you do not ask it now, you will soon be caught. You will go to college, get married, have children, husbands, wives, responsibilities, earn a livelihood, and then you will grow old and die. That is what happens to people. We have to ask now why we have lost this extraordinary feeling for beauty, when we see flowers, when we hear birds? Why do we lose the sense of the beautiful? I think we lose it primarily because we are so concerned with ourselves. We have an image of ourselves.

Do you know what an image is? It is something carved by the hand, out of stone, out of marble, and this stone carved by the hand is put in a temple and worshipped. But it is still handmade, an image made by man. You also have an image about yourself, not made by the hand, but made by the mind, by thought, by experience, by knowledge, by your struggle, by all the conflicts and miseries of your life. As you grow older that image becomes stronger, larger, all-demanding and insistent. The more you listen, act, have your existence in that image, the less you see beauty, feel joy at something beyond the little promptings of that image.

The reason you lose this quality of fullness is because you are so self-concerned. Do you know what that phrase 'to be self-concerned' means? It is to be occupied with oneself, to be occupied with one's capacities whether they are good or bad, with what your neighbours think of you, whether you have a good job, whether you are going to become an important man, or be thrown aside by society. You are always struggling in the office, at home, in the fields; wherever you are, whatever you do, you are always in conflict, and you do not seem to be able to get out of conflict; not being able to get out of it, you create the image of a perfect state, of heaven, of God—again another image made by the mind. You have other images deeper down, and they are always in conflict with each other. So the more you are in conflict—and conflict will always exist so long as you have images, opinions, concepts, ideas about yourself—the greater will be the struggle.

So the question is: Is it possible to live in this world without an image about yourself? You function as a doctor, a scientist, a teacher, a physicist. You use that function to create the image about yourself, and so, using function, you create conflict in functioning, in doing. I wonder if you understand this? You know, if you dance well, if you play an instrument, a violin, a veena, you use the instrument or the dance to create the image about yourself to feel how marvellous you are, how wonderfully well you play or dance.

You use the dancing, the playing of the instrument, in order to enrich your own image of yourself. And that is how you live, creating, strengthening that image of yourself. So there is more conflict; the mind gets dull and occupied with itself; and it loses the sense of beauty, of joy, of clear thinking.

I think it is part of education to function without creating images. You then function without the battle, the inward struggle that goes on within yourself.

There is no end to education. It is not that you read a book, pass an examination, and finish with education. The whole of life, from the moment you are born till the moment you die is a process of learning. Learning has no end and that is the timeless quality of learning. And you cannot learn if you are in battle, if you are in conflict with yourself, with your neighbour, with society. You are always in conflict with society, with your neighbour as long as there is an image. But if you are learning about the mechanics of putting together that image, then you will see that you can look at the sky, then you can look at the river and the raindrops on the leaf, feel the cool air of a morning and the fresh breeze among the leaves. Then life has an extraordinary meaning—life in itself, not the significance given by the image to life—life itself has an extraordinary meaning.

Student: When you are looking at a flower, what is your relationship with the flower?

Krishnamurti: You look at a flower, and what is your relationship to the flower? Do you look at the flower or do you think you are looking at the flower? You see the difference? Are you actually looking at the flower, or you think you ought to look at the flower, or are you looking at the flower with an image you have about the flower—the image being that it is a rose? The word is the image, the word is knowledge, and therefore you are looking at that flower with the word, the symbol, with knowledge, and therefore you are not looking at the flower. Or are you looking at it with a mind that is thinking about something else?

When you look at a flower without the word, without the image, and with a mind that is completely attentive, then what is the relationship between you and the flower? Have you ever done it? Have you ever looked at a flower without saying 'That is a rose'? Have you ever looked at a flower completely, with total attention in which there is no word, no symbol, no naming of the flower and, therefore, complete attention? Until you do that, you have no relationship with the flower. To have any relationship with another or with the rock or with the leaf, one has to watch and to observe with complete attention. Then your relationship to that which you see is entirely different. Then there is no observer at all. There is only that. If you so observe, then there is no opinion, no judgment. It is what it is. Have you understood? Will you do it? Look at a flower that way. Do it, sir, don't talk about it, but do it.

S: If you had lots of time, how would you spend it, sir?

K: I would do what I am doing. You see, if you love what you are doing, then you have all the leisure that you need in your life. Do you understand what I have said? You asked me what I would do if I had leisure. I said, I would do what I am doing, which is to go around different parts of the world, to talk, to see people, and so on. I do it because I love to do it, not because I talk to a great many people and feel that I am very important. When you feel very important, you do not love what you are doing; you love yourself and not what you are doing. So your concern should be not with what I am doing, but with what you are going to do. Right? I have told you what I am doing. Now you tell me what you will do when you have plenty of leisure.

S: I would get bored, sir.

K: You would get bored. Quite right. That is what most people are.

S: How do I get rid of this boredom, sir?

K: Wait, listen! Most people are bored. Why? You asked how to get rid of boredom. Now find out. When you are by yourself for half an hour, you are bored. So you pick up a book, chatter, look at a magazine, go to a cinema, talk, do something. You occupy your mind with something. This is an escape from yourself. You have asked a question; now pay attention to what is being said. You get bored because you find yourself with yourself, and you have never found yourself with yourself. Therefore you get bored. You say: 'Is that all I am? I am so small; I am so worried; I want to escape from all that.' What you are is very boring so you run away. But if you say, 'I am not going to be bored, I am going to find out why I am like this, I want to see what I am like actually', then it is like looking at yourself in a mirror. There you see very clearly what you are, what your face looks like. Then you say that you do not like your face, that you must be beautiful, you must look like a cinema actress. But if you were to look at yourself and say, 'Yes, that is what I am: my nose is not very straight, my eyes are rather small, my hair is straight.' You accept it. When you see what you are, there is no boredom. Boredom comes in only when you reject what you see and want to be something else. In the same way, when you can look at yourself inside and see exactly what you are, the seeing of it is not boring. It is extraordinarily interesting, because the more you see of it, the more there is to see. You can go deeper and deeper and wider and there is no end to it. In that there is no boredom. If you can do that, then what you do is what you love to do, and when you love to do a thing, time does not exist. When you love to plant trees, you water them, look after them, protect them. When you know what you really love to do, you will see the days are too short. So you have to find out for yourself from now on what you love to do, what you really want to do, not just be concerned with a career.

S: How do you find out what you love to do, sir?

K: How do you find out what you love to do? You have to understand that it may be different from what you want to do. You may want to become a lawyer, because your father is a lawyer or because you see that by becoming a lawyer you can earn more money. Then you do not love what you do because you have a motive for doing something that will give you profit, that will make you famous. But if you love something, there is no motive. You do not use what you are doing for your own self-importance.

To find out what you love to do is one of the most difficult things. That is part of education. To find that out you have to go into yourself very very deeply. It is not very easy. You may say: 'I want to be a lawyer', and you struggle to be a lawyer, and then suddenly you find you do not want to be a lawyer. You would like to paint. But it is too late. You are already married. You already have a wife and children. You cannot give up your career, your responsibilities. So you feel frustrated, unhappy. Or you may say, 'I really would like to paint', and you devote all your life to it, and suddenly find you are not a good painter and that what you really want to do is to be a pilot.

Right education is not to help you to find careers; for god's sake, throw that out of the window. Education is not merely gathering information from a teacher or learning mathematics from a book or learning historical dates of kings and customs. Education is to help you to understand problems as they arise, and that requires a good mind—a mind that reasons, a mind that is sharp, a mind that has no belief. For belief is not fact. A man who believes in God is as superstitious as a man who does not believe in God. To find out, you have to reason and you cannot reason if you already have an opinion, if you are prejudiced, if your mind has already come to a conclusion. So you need a good mind, a sharp, clear, definite, precise, healthy mind—not a believing mind, not a mind that follows authority. Right education is to help you to find out for yourself what you really—with all your heart—love to do. It does not matter what it is, whether it is to cook or to be a gardener, but it is something in which you have put your mind, your heart. Then you are really efficient, without becoming brutal. And this school should be a place where you are helped to find out for yourself through discussion, through listening, through silence—to find out right through your life—what you really love to do.

S: Sir, how can we know ourselves?

K: That is a very good question. Listen to me carefully. How do you know what you are? You understand my question? You look into the mirror for the first time and after a few days or few weeks, you look again and say, 'That is me again.' Right? So, by looking at the mirror every day, you begin to know your own face, and you say: 'That is me.' Now can you in the same way know what you are by watching yourself? Can you watch your gestures, the way you walk, the way you talk, the way you behave, whether you are hard, cruel, rough, patient? Then you begin to know yourself. You know yourself by watching yourself in the mirror of what you are doing, what you are thinking, what you are feeling. That is the mirror—the feeling, the doing, the thinking. And in that mirror you begin to watch yourself. The mirror says, this is the fact. But you do not like the fact, so you want to alter it; you start distorting it, you do not see it as it is.

You learn when there is attention and silence. Learning is when you have silence and give complete attention. In that state you begin to learn. Now sit very quietly, not because I am asking you to sit quietly, but because that is the way to learn. Sit very quietly and be still not only physically, not only in your body, but also in your mind. Be very still and then in that stillness, attend. Attend to the sounds outside this building, the cock crowing, the birds, somebody coughing, somebody leaving. Listen first to the things outside you, then listen to what is going on in your mind. And you will then see, if you listen very very attentively, in that silence, that the outside sound and the inside sound are the same.

From Commentaries on Living Second Series, *Chapter 2*

Conditioning

HE WAS VERY concerned with helping humanity, with doing good works, and was active in various social-welfare organizations. He said he had literally never taken a long holiday, and that since his graduation from college he had worked constantly for the betterment of man. Of course he wasn't taking any money for the work he was doing. His work had always been very important to him, and he was greatly attached to what he did. He had become a first-class social worker, and he loved it. But he had heard something in one of the talks about the various kinds of escape that condition the mind, and he wanted to talk things over.

'Do you think being a social worker is conditioning? Does it only bring about further conflict?'

Let us find out what we mean by conditioning. When are we aware that we are conditioned? Are we ever aware of it? Are you aware that you are conditioned, or are you only aware of conflict, of struggle at various levels of your being? Surely, we are aware, not of our conditioning, but only of conflict, of pain and pleasure.

'What do you mean by conflict?'

Every kind of conflict: the conflict between nations, between various social groups, between individuals, and the conflict within oneself. Is not conflict inevitable as long as there is no integration between the actor and his action, between challenge and response? Conflict is our problem, is it not? Not any one particular conflict, but all conflict: the struggle between ideas, beliefs, ideologies, between the opposites. If there were no conflict there would be no problems.

'Are you suggesting that we should all seek a life of isolation, of contemplation?'

Contemplation is arduous, it is one of the most difficult things to understand. Isolation, though each one is consciously or unconsciously seeking it in his own way, does not solve our problems; on the contrary, it increases them. We are trying to understand what are the factors of conditioning that bring further conflict. We are only aware of conflict, of pain and pleasure, and we are not aware of our conditioning. What makes for conditioning?

'Social or environmental influences: the society in which we were born, the culture in which we have been raised, economic and political pressures, and so on.'

That is so; but is that all? These influences are our own product, are they not? Society is the outcome of man's relationship with man, which is fairly obvious. This relationship is one of use, of need, of comfort, of gratification, and it creates influences, values that bind us. The binding is our conditioning. By our own thoughts and actions we are bound; but we are not aware that we are bound, we are only aware of the conflict of pleasure and pain. We never seem to go beyond this; and if we do, it is only into further conflict. We are not aware of our conditioning, and until we are, we can only produce further conflict and confusion.

'How is one to be aware of one's conditioning?'

It is possible only by understanding another process, the process of attachment. If we can understand why we are attached, then perhaps we can be aware of our conditioning.

'Isn't that rather a long way round to come to a direct question?'

Is it? Just try to be aware of your conditioning. You can only know it indirectly, in relation to something else. You cannot be aware of your conditioning as an abstraction, for then it is merely verbal, without much significance. We are only aware of conflict. Conflict exists when there is no integration between challenge and response. This conflict is the result of our conditioning. Conditioning is attachment: attachment to work, to tradition, to property, to people, to ideas, and so on. If there were no attachment, would there be conditioning? Of course not. So why are we attached? I am attached to my country because through identification with it I become somebody. I identify myself with my work, and the work becomes important. I am my family, my property; I am attached to them. The object of attachment offers me the means of escape from my own emptiness. Attachment is escape, and it is escape that strengthens conditioning. If I am attached to you, it is because you have become the means of escape from myself; therefore you are very important to me and I must possess you, hold on to you. You become the conditioning factor, and escape is the conditioning. If we can be aware of our escapes, we can then perceive the factors, the influences that make for conditioning.

'Am I escaping from myself through social work?'

Are you attached to it, bound to it? Would you feel lost, empty, bored, if you did not do social work?

'I am sure I would.'

Attachment to your work is your escape. There are escapes at all the levels of our being. You escape through work, another through drink, another through religious ceremonies, another through knowledge, another through God, and still another is addicted to amusement. All escapes are the same, there is no superior or inferior escape. God and drink are on the same level as long as they are escapes from what we are. When we are aware of our escapes, only then can we know of our conditioning.

'What shall I do if I cease to escape through social work? Can I do anything without escaping? Is not all my action a form of escape from what I am?'

Is this question merely verbal, or does it reflect an actuality, a fact that you are experiencing? If you did not escape, what would happen? Have you ever tried it?

'What you are saying is so negative, if I may say so. You don't offer any substitute for work.'

Is not all substitution another form of escape? When one particular form of activity is not satisfactory or brings further conflict, we turn to another. To replace one activity by another without understanding escape is rather futile, is it not? It is these escapes and our attachment to them that make for conditioning. Conditioning brings problems, conflict. It is conditioning that prevents our understanding of the challenge; being conditioned, our response must inevitably create conflict.

'How can one be free from conditioning?'

Only by understanding, being aware of our escapes. Our attachment to a person, to work, to an ideology, is the conditioning factor; this is the thing we have to understand, and not seek a better or more intelligent escape. All escapes are unintelligent, as they inevitably bring about conflict. To cultivate detachment is another form of escape, of isolation; it is attachment to an abstraction, to an ideal called detachment. The ideal is fictitious, ego-made, and becoming the ideal is an escape from what is. There is the understanding of what is, an adequate action towards what is, only when the mind is no longer seeking any escape. The very thinking about what is, is an escape from what is. Thinking about the problem is escape from the problem; for thinking is the problem, and the only problem. The mind, unwilling to be what it is, fearful of what it is, seeks these various escapes; and the way of escape is thought. As long as there is thinking, there must be escapes, attachments, which only strengthen conditioning.

Freedom from conditioning comes with the freedom from thinking. When the mind is utterly still, only then is there freedom for the real to be.

Saanen, 24 July 1973

Questioner: Would you go into the question of earning a livelihood because that requires capacity, that requires thought, that requires knowledge? Would you go into that?

Krishnamurti: As the culture and the civilisation of which we are part now exist, we are brought up to work for our life; work, work, work, all day long. Right? What a horror it is! To be told, to be under somebody, to be directed, to be insulted, to be beaten down. That is the culture in which we have grown, in which you have been moulded. And to conform to that mould, we are educated. We are educated mainly to acquire knowledge, to cultivate memory so as to earn a livelihood. That is the primary function of education as it is now. And therefore in that education there is conformity, competition, imitation, ambition, success. Success implies more money, better position, a better house, and so on. That is the structure in which we have been brought up. Knowledge and the cultivation of memory have become tremendously important to function in this field, and you totally discard the rest of existence. That is a fact.

Now you say, 'How am I to earn a livelihood, though I need knowledge, and yet I see the limitation of knowledge?' I need to earn bread and butter, I need to have food, clothes, and shelter; whether the State supplies it, or I work for it, it is the same thing.

Knowledge is very limited; it is mechanical, and we try to escape through religions, through sex, through idiosyncrasies, through neuroticism, through the desire to fulfil ourselves in some-thing apart from this world. But yet what am I to do? How am I to live in harmony, having knowledge, functioning in knowledge, and also freeing the mind from this mechanical process of learning, so that the two run together? So that the mind lives, going to the fac-tory, working without competition, because it is not concerned with achieving a position. It is only concerned with achieving a liveli-hood. I don't know if you see the difference. Also it sees very clearly the freedom from the known, which is the knowledge, which is the past. Can these two streams move together harmoniously all the time? That is our problem. Not the problem of earning more, and more, and more, which society wants, which is consumerism, com-mercialism—all the tricks played on the mind to make you buy, buy, buy. I won't. I see the falseness. And I see at the same time the freedom, from the known that is knowledge. Can these two work together all the time, so that there is no friction?

Now what is harmony? You understand, that is the prob-lem. I see I must earn a livelihood. I won't fight, I won't compete, I will work because I have put my brain, my capacity into it, there-fore I work very efficiently because I have no psychological prob-lems with work; I will not compete with anybody, therefore my capacity, my energy, my way of writing, producing, whatever it is, is complete. Therefore there is no conflict, there is no wastage of en-ergy. I hope you see this.

And so I am asking: What is harmony? I say there must be harmony between the two. Now what is this harmony? Can har-mony, this sense of balance, this sense of sanity, this sense of feeling whole—work, knowledge, and freedom from knowledge; that is the whole—can that sense of wholeness be brought about by thought, by investigation, by reading, by searching, by asking? Or does this wholeness come about through thought? Thought cannot bring it—obviously. So seeing that thought cannot bring it about, seeing that I can work efficiently, with full energy because I have no psychological problems and therefore I am only working to earn a livelihood for self-sufficiency, I see the whole thing must work together. And it can only work together when there is intelligence. So intelligence is harmony.

It is intelligence that says: work only for a livelihood, not for ambition, not for competition, not to succeed and all the rest of it. Work. That is life. It is the intelligence that has told me, not a conclusion. And also intelligence says to me: freedom is necessary. So intelligence says there must be harmony. So intelligence brings about this harmony. It is not an outside agency or thought that brings about this harmony. Now I don't know if you have noticed that thought is always outside. Thought is always from the outside. I was told the other day that in the Eskimo language thought means outside. So thought cannot possibly produce harmony, balance, this sense of wholeness.

But what brings about this total sense of integrity, this sense of sanity, wholeness? Intelligence—which is not the intellectual acceptance of an idea; it is not the product of reason, logic, though reason and logic must exist, but it is not the result of that; it is the perception of truth from which arises wisdom. Wisdom is the daughter of truth, and intelligence is the daughter of wisdom—right? Do you see it? Do work at this. You understand? Just look at it, drink it. And then it is there; you don't have to struggle, read books, and go through all the tortures of life.

Saanen, 3 August 1973

Krishnamurti: What am I to do, living in this world, having to earn a livelihood, and to have clothes, food, shelter, and leisure? What am I to do knowing the cause of this loneliness, which is, let us say, ambition, the competitive spirit? How am I to live without ambition, without the competition in this world? Come on, this is your life.

Questioner: What is the quality of seriousness?

K: I am asking something, you answer something else. I am asking how I am to live in this world, earn a livelihood, and yet not be ambitious, not be competitive, not conform. How am I to live, because I feel terribly lonely and I see that loneliness has been brought about by competition, ambition, and so on. That is the structure of society in which I live, that is the culture. What am I to do?

Q: I must see my real needs.

K: Not 'must'. Then you are talking of ideas. Have you solved the problem of ambition by halving your needs? I need four pairs of trousers, half a dozen shirts, and half a dozen shoes, or whatever it is—that's all I need. But I am still ambitious. Move away!

Q: How am I to change my action?

K: I am going to show it to you. Have a little patience, go with the speaker step by step, you will find out for yourself. Look, I am going to repeat the question again. I am lonely, this loneliness has been brought about by self-centred activity, and one of its forms is ambition, greed, envy, competitiveness, imitation. I have to live in this society that makes me conform, be ambitious, encourages hypocrisy and all the rest of it. How am I to learn a livelihood and yet not be ambitious, because ambition is a form of isolation? I am lonely—you understand—therefore how am I to live without ambition in this world? And all of you are ambitious.

Q: Give all your mind and energy to understand it.

K: I give up! You don't apply, you don't say, 'Look, I am ambitious—I am ambitious in ten different ways—spiritually, psychologically, physically, and so on. I am ambitious. I have created this society through ambition, and that ambition has brought about this sense of isolation, which is loneliness, and I have to live in this world, and I don't want to be lonely. It doesn't mean anything. Therefore I am asking, how am I to live in this world without ambition, live amongst you who are ambitious, but I don't want to be ambitious? How am I to live with you?'

Don't you know the danger of ambition?. . . This is such a lovely world! . . . I am showing you that you are ambitious. You don't face that question, you go all round it.

Q: What is ambition?

K: Trying to be something other than what you are. Just listen. I have said ambition is to transform what you are into something that you are not. That is one part of ambition. Ambition is to try to achieve something that you think is desirable, something that you think will give you power, position, prestige. Ambition is to write something and hope that it will sell a million copies, and so on, and on and on. And that is the society in which I am forced to live. And

I realize that has brought loneliness to me, and I see how tremendously destructive this loneliness is because it prevents my relationship with another. So I see the destructive nature of it, then what am I to do?

Q: Find a person who is not ambitious.

K: Aren't you ambitious? Have I to go out and find somebody else? What are you all talking about? You are not serious.

I am asking myself: I am lonely—ambition, greed, competition have brought about this loneliness—and I see the destructive nature of it. It really prevents affection, care, love, and to me that is tremendously important. Loneliness is terrible, it is destructive, it is poisonous. Now how am I to live with you who are ambitious, because I have to live with you; I have to earn my livelihood. What am I to do?. . .

You don't understand. I am boiling. I am passionate to understand this problem. It is burning me up, because that is my whole life and you are playing with it. I am lonely, desperate, and I see how destructive it is, and I want to resolve it. And yet I have to live with you, live with this world that is ambitious, greedy, violent. What am I to do? I will show you. But showing is not the same thing as you doing it. I'll show it.

Can I live in a world that is tremendously ambitious, and therefore deceitful, dishonest? Now how am I to live there, in that world, because I don't want to be ambitious. I see what the result of ambition is—loneliness, despair, ugliness, violence, and so on. Now I say to myself, how am I to live with you who are ambitious? And am I ambitious? Not somebody else, not the world, because the world is me; I am the world, and that's to me a burning reality, not just a phrase. So am I ambitious? Now I am going to learn. I am going to observe, and find out if I am ambitious, not just in one direction, my whole life. Not the ambition to have a bigger house, the ambition to be successful, the ambition to achieve a result, money, but also the ambition to transform 'what is' into the perfect state. I am ugly and I want to transform that into the most beautiful state. All that and more is ambition. And I watch it. That's my life, you understand? I am going to watch it with passion, not just sit down and discuss it. I am watching it night and day because I have realized the truth that loneliness is the most terrible thing because it is most destructive in relationship. And human beings cannot live by themselves. Life is relationship. Life is action in that relationship. If in that relationship there is isolation there is total inaction. I realize that, not verbally, but as a burning reality.

Now I am watching. Am I ambitious to transform 'what is' into 'what should be', the ideal? You understand? That's a form of ambition to change what I am into what I should be. Am I doing that? That is, are *you* doing that? When I say 'I', I am talking about you. Don't just escape. I am talking about you when I talk about me, because you are me. Because you are the world, and I am part of that world.

So I watch, and I say, yes, I want to change 'what is' into 'what should be'. And I realize how absurd that is. It is a part of ambition given to me by education, culture, tradition. In school 'A' is better than 'B', copy 'A'—you know all that business. The religions have said, change from what you are to what you should be. So I realize the falseness of it, and I totally discard it. I will not touch it. So I accept 'what is'. Wait a minute. I see 'what is', and I see 'what is' isn't good enough. So how am I to transform it without the ambition of changing it into something?

Now I see what it is; I am greedy. I don't want to transform it into non-greed. I am violent; I don't want to transform it into non-violence. But that violence must undergo a radical change. Now what am I to do with it? What is my mind to do, which has been trained, educated, disciplined to be ambitious, violent? When I realize that to change that into something else is still violence, I won't proceed along those lines. And I am left with 'what is', which is violence. So what takes place? How am I to observe it, how is the mind to observe it without wanting to change it?

How is the mind to change this educated, sophisticated ambition so completely that there is not a breath of ambition? All day I am watching how my ambition is active. Because I am very serious, because the loneliness is a terrible thing in relationship, and man can't live without relationship. He may pretend, he may say he loves, but still fight with another. So how is the mind to transform totally the thing called ambition? Any form of exercise of will is still ambition. All this is observation. I see that any form of exercise of will to transform 'what is' is another form of ambition. I have discovered that. The discovery of it has given me energy, so that I can discard will. The mind says that is finished, I will never in any circumstances exercise will—because that is part of ambition.

And I see that conformity is one of the educated reactions of the culture in which I live—the conformity of long hair, short hair, short trousers, a short skirt, conform, outwardly and inwardly conform; become a Buddhist, a Catholic, a Moslem; conform. I have been taught from childhood to conform. I am forced, educated, compelled to conform. What takes place when I conform? There is struggle, isn't there? Conflict—I am this, and you want me to be that. So there is conflict, there is loss of energy, there is fear that I am not what you expect me to be. So conformity, will, desire to change 'what is', is all part of ambition. I am observing this. So I observe and I say, 'I will not conform.' I understand what conformity is: I am conforming when I put on trousers; I am conforming when I keep to the left or right side of the road; I am conforming when I learn a language; I conform when I shake hands. So I am conforming in a certain direction, at certain levels, and at other levels I am not conforming—because that is part of isolation. So what has happened? What has happened to the mind that has observed the activities of ambition—conformity, will, the desire to change 'what is' into 'what should be', and so on? Those are all the activities of ambition that have produced this sense of desperate loneliness. So all kinds of neurotic activities take place. And as I have observed it, watched it, without doing a thing about it, then out of that observation the activity of ambition has come to an end because the mind has become extraordinarily sensitive to ambition. It is as if it cannot tolerate ambition, therefore becoming very sensitive it has become extraordinarily intelligent. It says, 'How am I to live in this world being highly sensitive, intelligent, and therefore with no ambition?'

How am I to live with you who are ambitious? Have we any relationship with each other? You are ambitious, and I am not. Or you are not, I am—it doesn't matter which way. What is our relationship?

Q: There is no relationship.

K: Therefore what am I to do? Because I realize living is relationship. You are ambitious, and perhaps I am not. And I see that we have no relationship because you are going that way and I am going there, or I am stationary and you are moving away. What is our relationship? And yet I cannot live by myself.

Look at it, absorb it, smell it, taste it, and then you will answer it. What am I to do, living in this world, which is made up of ambition, greed, hypocrisy, violence; trying to change this into that, you know all that is happening. And I see that all leads to loneliness and that destroys relationship. . . . The mind has come to the point when it has to face a crowd, a civilisation, a world in which the poison of ambition is rampant. And this mind will not tolerate psychologically and physically any form of ambition, and yet it has to live here. What is it to do?

I am asking you. I'll say I am ambitious; you are not ambitious; what is our relationship?

Q: There is no relationship.

K: There is no relationship? What takes place?

Q: Complete isolation.

K: You have missed the point, sir, which is, when the mind has observed the activity of ambition, when the mind has observed all this and seen the falseness and therefore the truth of it, the mind becomes very sensitive to see all the currents of ambition. Therefore the mind is intelligent. It has become intelligent in the sense that through observation of the current and the subtleties of ambition, it realizes ambition is poison. The mind being highly sensitive to ambition and therefore intelligent, has to live with you. It can't isolate itself. Because it sees that isolation has brought this mess about. Now how is it to live with you? You are going that way, and the non-ambitious person may not be going that way, or going in any direction.

Such a mind is not isolated, is it? Isolation, which is loneliness, takes place when there are all the activities of ambition. When there are no activities of ambition, there is no loneliness. I have taken one example of the cause of loneliness. If I understand one cause of loneliness I have understood all the other causes. Because in this one cause is included conformity, in this one cause is included will, wanting to change this to that in order to become something, in order to be greater, nobler, wiser, more rich, and so on. All that I discover in this one act of ambition.

To ME IT is an appalling thing to be ambitious. I have realized it, and I see the ugliness, the falseness of it, not verbally but actually. Therefore what takes place? It is like seeing a precipice; that is not an abstraction; when I see a precipice I move away from it, if I am sane. Then am I lonely? Of course not. I am self-sufficient. You understand? My relationship with you then is that I am self-sufficient and you are not, therefore you are going to exploit me. You are going to use me to satisfy yourself, and I say, 'Don't do it, it is a waste of time.' So relationship based on loneliness is one thing, but relationship based on non-loneliness, on complete self-sufficiency, is another.

We have come to a marvellous point. Relationship born out of loneliness leads to great misery. Just listen to this. Don't say, 'I must live that way.' It's like smelling a flower; just smell it, you can't do anything about it, you can't create a flower, you can only destroy it. Therefore just smell it, look at it, the beauty, the petals, the delicacy, the extraordinary quality of gentleness; you know what a flower is. In the same way just look at this, listen to this. Relationship out of loneliness leads to conflict, misery, divorce, fights, wrangles, sexual insufficiency. Out of that loneliness all the misery comes in relationship. Then what takes place when there is no loneliness, when there is complete self-sufficiency, no dependency? You understand? When there is no dependency what takes place? I love you, you may not love me, I love you—that's good enough. You understand? I don't want your response that you love me also. I don't care. Like the flower, it is there for you to look at it, to smell, see the beauty of it. It doesn't say, 'Love me.' It is there. Therefore it is related to everything. You understand? Oh, for god's sake get this. And in the great depth and beauty of sufficiency—in which there is no loneliness, no ambition—there is really love, and love has relationship with nature. If you want it, there it is; if you don't want it, it doesn't matter. That's the beauty of it.

From Truth and Actuality, Chapter 10, Saanen, 25 July 1976

Right Livelihood

Questioner: Is a motive necessary in business? What is the right motive in earning a livelihood?

Krishnamurti: What do you think is the right livelihood?—not what is the most convenient, not what is the most profitable, enjoyable, or gainful; but what is the right livelihood? Now, how will you find out what is right? The word *right* means correct, accurate. It cannot be accurate if you do something for profit or pleasure. This is a complex thing. Everything that thought has put together is reality. This tent [in which the discussion is taking place] has been put together by thought, it is a reality. The tree has not been put together by thought, but it is a reality. Illusions are reality—the illusions that one has, imagination, all that is reality. And the action from those illusions is neurotic, which is also reality. So when you ask this question, 'What is the right livelihood', you must understand what reality is. Reality is not truth.

  Now what is correct action in this reality? And how will you discover what is right in this reality?—discover for yourself, not be told. So we have to find out what is the accurate, correct, right action, or right livelihood in the world of reality, and reality includes illusion. Don't escape, don't move away, belief is an illusion, and the activities of belief are neurotic; nationalism and all the rest of it is another form of reality, but an illusion. So taking all that as reality, what is the right action there?

Who is going to tell you? Nobody, obviously. But when you see reality without illusion, the very perception of that reality is your intelligence—isn't it?—in which there is no mixture of reality and illusion. So when there is observation of reality, the reality of the tree, the reality of the tent, reality that thought has put together, including visions, illusions, when you see all that reality, the very perception of that is your intelligence—isn't it? So your intelligence says what you are going to do. I wonder if you understand this? Intelligence is to perceive what is and what is not—to perceive 'what is' and see the reality of 'what is', which means you don't have any psychological involvement, any psychological demands, which are all forms of illusion. To see all that is intelligence; and that intelligence will operate wherever you are. Therefore that will tell you what to do.

Then what is truth? What is the link between reality and truth? The link is this intelligence. Intelligence that sees the totality of reality and therefore doesn't carry it over to truth. And the truth then operates on reality through intelligence.

Ojai, 3 April 1977

When there is no conflict inside, there is no conflict outside, because there is no division between the inner and the outer. It's like ebb and flow, the sea coming in and the sea going out, . . . and if I had to earn a livelihood, what should I do, having psychologically no conflict of any kind? Do you know what that means? Because there is no conflict there is no ambition, no desire to be something. Inwardly there is something that is absolutely inviolable, that cannot be touched, that cannot be damaged; then I don't depend, psychologically on another. Therefore there is no conformity.

So not having all that, then I will do what I can in the world, be a gardener, a cook, anything. But you're so heavily conditioned to success, and failure. Success in the world, money, position, prestige, you know, all that, and that's what we are struggling for. Human consciousness is heavily conditioned to success, and the fear of failure. To be something, not only outwardly but inwardly. That's why you accept all the gurus, because you hope they'll lead you to some illumination, some kind of illusory nonsense. Not that there is not something absolutely true, but nobody can lead you to it.

So our whole consciousness, or most of it, is conditioned to accept, to live a life of constant struggle, because we want to achieve, we want to become, we want to play a certain part, we want to fulfil, which all implies the denial of 'what is' and the acceptance of 'what should be'. If you observe violence, the word *violence* is already contaminated—the very word—because there are people who approve of it, people who don't approve of it; it's already warped. And the whole philosophy of non-violence politically, religiously, and all the rest of it. There is violence and its opposite, non-violence. The opposite has its root in 'what is'. But we think by having an opposite, by some extraordinary method or means, we'll get rid of 'what is'—that is: 'what is' and 'what should be'. To achieve 'what should be', you need time. See what we go through, the misery, the conflict, the absurdity of all this. 'What is', is violence, and 'what should be' is non-violence. So we say we need time to achieve non-violence, that we must make an effort, must struggle to be non-violent. That's the philosophy, that's the conditioning, that's the tradition.

Now can you put away the opposite and just look at violence, which is a fact. The non-violence is not a fact. Non-violence is an idea, a concept, a conclusion. But the *fact* is violence, that you're angry, that you hate somebody, that you want to hurt people; anger, jealousy, all that is the implication of violence. Now can you observe that fact without introducing its opposite. You understand? Then you have the energy—which is being wasted in trying to achieve the opposite—to observe 'what is'. In that observation there is no conflict.

So what will a man do who has understood this extraordinary complex existence based on violence, conflict, struggle; who is actually, not theoretically but actually free, which means no conflict? What shall he do in the world? Will you ask this question—whether you are inwardly, psychologically completely free from conflict? Will you?

Society is based on conflict. But society is what you have made of it; you are responsible for it, because you are greedy, envious, violent, and society is what you are. So there is no difference between you and society. These are facts. But you separate yourself from society and say, 'I am different from society', which is such nonsense. If there is complete transformation of the structure of society—which is violence, immorality, and all the rest of it—in *you*,

you affect the consciousness of society. And when you are so free inwardly, do you ever ask that question, 'What shall I do in the outward world?' Do answer it yourself, find out what the answer is for yourself, because inwardly you have then completely transformed something that man is conditioned to—that constant battle, battle, battle.

From Commentaries on Living Third Series, *Chapter 48*

What Am I To Do?

THE WIND WAS blowing fresh and cool. It was not the dry air of the surrounding semi-desert but came from the mountains far away. Those mountains were among the highest in the world, a great chain of them running from north-west to south-east. They were massive and sublime, an incredible sight when you saw them in the early morning, before the sun was on the sleeping land. Their towering peaks, glowing a delicate rose, were startlingly clear against the pale blue sky. As the sun climbed higher the plains were covered with long shadows. Soon those mysterious peaks would disappear in the clouds, but before they withdrew, they would leave their blessing on the valleys, the rivers, and the towns. Though you could no longer see them, you could feel that they were there, silent, immense, and timeless.

A beggar was coming down the road, singing; he was blind, and a child was leading him. People passed him by, and occasionally someone would drop a coin or two into the tin he was holding in one hand; but he went on with his song, heedless of the rattle of the coins. A servant came out of a big house, dropped a coin in the tin, muttered something, and went back again, shutting the gate behind him. The parrots were off for the day in their crazy and noisy flight. They would go to the fields and the woods, but towards evening they would return for the night to the trees along the road; it was safer there, though the street-lights were almost among the leaves. Many other birds seemed to remain all day in the town and on a big lawn some of them were trying to catch the sleepy worms. A boy went by, playing his flute. He was lean and barefooted; there was a swagger in his walk, and his feet didn't seem to mind where they trod. He was the flute, and the song was in his eyes. Walking behind him, you felt that he was the first boy with a flute in all the world. And, in a way, he was; for he paid no attention to the car that rushed past, nor to the policeman standing at the corner, heavy with sleep, nor to the woman with a bundle on her head. He was lost to the world but his song went on.

And now the day had begun.

The room was not very large, and the few who had come rather crowded it. They were of all ages. There was an old man with his very young daughter, a married couple, and a college student. They evidently didn't know each other, and each was eager to talk about his own problem, but without wanting to interfere with the others. The little girl sat beside her father, shy and very quiet; she must have been about ten. She had on fresh clothes, and there was a flower in her hair. We all sat for a while without saying a word. The college student waited for age to speak, but the old man preferred to let others speak first. At last, rather nervously, the young man began.

'I am now in my last year at college, where I have been studying engineering, but somehow I don't seem to be interested in any particular career. I simply don't know what I want to do. My father, who is a lawyer, doesn't care what I do as long as I do something of course; since I am studying engineering he would like me to be an engineer, but I have no real interest in it. I have told him this, but he says the interest will come once I get working at it for a livelihood. I have several friends who studied for different careers, and who are now earning their own way; but most of them are already becoming dull and weary, and what they will be like a few years hence, God only knows. I don't want to be like that—and I'm sure I will be, if I become an engineer. It isn't that I'm afraid of the exams, I can pass them easily enough, and I'm not boasting. I just don't want to be an engineer, and nothing else seems to interest me either. I have done a spot of writing, and have dabbled in painting but that kind of thing doesn't carry very far. My father is only concerned with pushing me into a job, and he could get me a good one; but I know what will happen to me if I accept it. I feel like throwing up everything and leaving college without waiting to take the final exams.'

That would be rather silly, wouldn't it? After all you are nearly through college; why not finish it? There's no harm in that, is there?

'I suppose not. But what am I to do then?'

Apart from the usual careers, what would you really like to do? You must have some interest, however vague it may be. Somewhere, deep down, you know what it is, don't you?

'You see, I don't want to become rich; I have no interest in raising a family, and I don't want to be a slave to a routine. Most of my friends who have jobs, or who have embarked upon a career, are tied to the office from morning till night; and what do they get out of it? A house, a wife, some children—and boredom. To me, this is really a frightening prospect, and I don't want to be caught in it; but I still don't know what to do.'

Since you have thought so much about all this, haven't you tried to find out where your real interest lies? What does your mother say?

'She doesn't care what I do as long as I am safe, which means being securely married and tied down; so she backs father up. On my walks I have thought a great deal about what I would really like to do, and I have talked it over with friends. But most of my friends are bent on some career or other, and it's no good talking to them. Once they are caught in a career, whatever it may be, they think it's the right thing to do—duty, responsibility, and all the rest of it. I just don't want to get caught in a similar treadmill that's all. But what is it I would really like to do? I wish I knew.'

Do you like people?

'In a vague sort of way. Why do you ask?'

Perhaps you might like to do something along the line of social work.

'Curious you should say that. I have thought of doing social work, and for a time I went around with some of those who have given their lives to it. Generally speaking, they are a dry, frustrated lot, frightfully concerned about the poor, and ceaselessly active in trying to improve social conditions, but unhappy inside. I know one young woman who would give her right arm to get married and lead a family life, but her idealism is destroying her. She's caught in the routine of doing good works, and has become dreadfully cheerful about her boredom. It's all idealism without flair, without inward joy.'

I suppose religion, in the accepted sense, means nothing to you?

'As a boy I often used to go with my mother to the temple, with its priests, prayers, and ceremonies, but I haven't been there for years.'

That too becomes a routine, a repetitious sensation, a living on words and explanations. Religion is something much more than all that. Are you adventurous?

'Not in the usual meaning of that word—mountain climbing, polar exploration, deep-sea diving, and so on. I'm not being superior, but to me there's something rather immature about all that. I could no more climb mountains than hunt whales.'

What about politics?

'The ordinary political game doesn't interest me. I have some Communist friends, and have read some of their stuff, and at one time I thought of joining the party; but I can't stomach their double talk, their violence and tyranny. These are the things they actually stand for, whatever may be their official ideology and their talk of peace. I went through that phase quickly.'

We have eliminated a great deal, haven't we? If you don't want to do any of these things, then what's left?

'I don't know. Am I still too young to know?'

It's not a matter of age, is it? Discontent is part of existence, but we generally find a way to tame it, whether through a career, through marriage, through belief, or through idealism and good works. One way or another, most of us manage to smother this flame of discontent, don't we? After successfully smothering it, we think at last we are happy—and we may be, at least for the time being. Now, instead of smothering this flame of discontent through some form of satisfaction, is it possible to keep it always burning? And is it then discontent?

'Do you mean I should remain as I am, dissatisfied with everything about me and within myself, and not seek some satisfying occupation that will let this fire burn out? Is that what you mean?'

We are discontented because we think we should be contented; the idea that we should be at peace with ourselves makes discontentment painful. You think you ought to be something, don't you?—a responsible person, a useful citizen, and all the rest of it. With the understanding of discontent, you may be these things and much more. But you want to do something satisfying, something that will occupy your mind and so put an end to this inner disturbance; isn't that so?

'It is in a way, but I now see what such occupation leads to.'

The occupied mind is a dull, routine mind; in essence it's mediocre. Because it's established in habit, in belief, in a respectable and profitable routine, the mind feels secure, both inwardly and outwardly; therefore it ceases to be disturbed. This is so, isn't it?

'In general, yes. But what am I to do?'

You may discover the solution if you go further into this feeling of discontent. Don't think about it in terms of being contented. Find out why it exists, and whether it shouldn't be kept burning. After all, you are not particularly concerned about earning a livelihood, are you?

'Quite bluntly, I am not. One can always live somehow or other.'

So that's not your problem at all. But you don't want to be caught in a routine, in the wheel of mediocrity; isn't that what you are concerned about?

'It looks like it, sir.'

Not to be thus caught demands hard work, incessant watching, it means coming to no conclusions from which to continue further thinking; for to think from a conclusion is not to think at all. It's because the mind starts from a conclusion, from a belief, from experience, from knowledge, that it gets caught in routine, in the net of habit, and then the fire of discontent is smothered.

'I see that you are perfectly right, and I now understand what it is that has really been on my mind. I don't want to be like those whose life is routine and boredom, and I say this without any sense of superiority. Losing oneself in various forms of adventure is equally meaningless; and I don't want to be merely contented either. I have begun to see, however vaguely, in a direction that I never knew even existed. Is this new direction what you were referring to the other day in your talk when you spoke of a state, or a movement, which is timeless and ever creative?'

Perhaps. Religion is not a matter of churches, temples, rituals, and beliefs; it's the moment-by-moment discovery of that movement, which may have any name, or no name.

'I'm afraid I have taken more than my share of the available time', he said, turning to the others. 'I hope you don't mind.'

'On the contrary', replied the old man, 'I for one have listened very attentively, and have profited a great deal; I, too, have seen something beyond my problem. In listening quietly to the troubles of another, our own burdens are sometimes lightened.'

He was silent for a minute or two, as if considering how to express what he wanted to say.

'Personally, I have reached an age', he went on, 'when I no longer ask what I am going to do; instead, I look back and consider what I have done with my life. I too went to college, but I was not as thoughtful as our young friend here. Upon graduating from college, I went in search of work, and once having found a job, I spent the next forty years and more in earning a livelihood and maintaining a rather large family. During all that time I was caught in the office routine to which you have referred, and in the habits of family life, and I know its pleasures and tribulations, its tears and passing joys. I have grown old with struggle and weariness, and in recent years there has been a fast decline. Looking back on all that, I now ask myself, 'What have you done with your life? Apart from your family and your job, what have you actually accomplished?'

The old man paused before answering his own question.

'Over the years, I joined various associations for the improvement of this and that; I belonged to several different religious groups, and left one for another; and I hopefully read the literature of the extreme left, only to find that their organization is as tyrannically authoritarian as the church. Now that I have retired, I can see that I have been living on the surface of life; I have merely drifted. Though I struggled a little against the strong current of society, in the end I was pulled along by it. But don't misunderstand me. I'm not shedding tears over the past; I don't bemoan the things that have been. I am concerned with the few years that I still have left. Between now and the fast-approaching day of my death, how am I to meet this thing called life? That is my problem.'

What we are is made up of what we have been; and what we have been also shapes the future, without definitely giving line and substance to every thought and action. The present is a movement of the past to the future.

'What has been my past? Practically nothing at all. There have been no great sins, no towering ambition, no overwhelming sorrow, no degrading violence. My life has been that of the average man, neither hot nor cold; it has been an even flow, a thoroughly mediocre life. I have built up a past in which there's nothing to be either proud or ashamed of. My whole existence has been dull and empty, without much meaning. It would have been the same, had I lived in a palace, or in a village hut. How easy it is to slip into the current of mediocrity! Now, my question is, can I stem in myself this current of mediocrity? Is it possible to break away from my pettily enlarging past?'

What is the past? When you use the word *past*, what does it signify?

'It seems to me that the past is chiefly a matter of association and memory.'

Do you mean the totality of memory, or just the memory of everyday incidents? Incidents that have no psychological significance, while they may be remembered, do not take root in the soil of the mind. They come and go; they do not occupy or burden the mind. Only those remain that have psychological significance. So what do you mean by the past? Is there a past that remains solid, immovable, from which you can cleanly and sharply break away?

'My past is made up of a multitude of little things put together, and its roots are shallow. A good shock like a strong wind, could blow it away.'

And you are waiting for the wind. Is that your problem?

'I'm not waiting for anything. But must I go on like this for the rest of my days? Can I not break away from the past?'

Again, what is the past from which you want to break away? Is the past static, or is it a living thing? If it's a living thing, how does it get its life? Through what means does it revive itself? If it's a living thing, can you break away from it? And who is the 'you' that wants to break away?

'Now I'm getting confused', he complained. 'I have asked a simple question, and you counter it by asking several more complicated ones. Would you kindly explain what you mean?'

You say, sir, that you want to be free from the past. What is this past?

'It consists of experiences and the memories one has of them.'

Now, these memories, you say, are on the surface, they are not deep-rooted. But may not some of them have roots deep in the unconscious?

'I don't think I have any deep-rooted memories. Tradition and belief have deep roots in many people, but I follow them only as a matter of social convenience. They don't play a very significant part in my life.'

If the past is to be dismissed so easily, there's no problem; if only the outer husk of the past remains, which can be brushed off at any time, then you have already broken away. But there's more to the problem than that, isn't there? How are you to break through your mediocre life? How are you to shatter the pettiness of the mind? Isn't this also your problem, sir? And surely, the 'how' in this case is a furtherance of inquiry, not the demand for a method. It's the practising of a method, based on the desire to succeed, with its fear and authority, that has brought about pettiness in the first place.

'I came with the intention of dispelling my past, which is without much significance, but I am being confronted with another problem.'

Why do you say that your past is without much significance?

'I have drifted on the surface of life, and when you drift, you can't have deep roots, even in your family. I see that to me life hasn't meant very much; I have done nothing with it. Only a few years are now left to me, and I want to stop drifting, I want to make something of what remains of my life. Is this at all possible?'

What do you want to make of your life? Doesn't the pattern of what you want to be evolve from what you have been? Surely, your pattern is a reaction from what has been; it is an outcome of the past.

'Then how am I to make anything of life?'

What do you mean by life? Can you act upon it? Or is life incalculable, and not to be held within the boundaries of the mind? Life is everything, isn't it? Jealousy, vanity, inspiration, and despair; social morality, and the virtue that is outside the realm of cultivated righteousness; knowledge gathered through the centuries; character, which is the meeting of the past with the present; organized beliefs, called religions, and the truth that lies beyond them; hate and affection; love and compassion, which are not within the field of the mind—all this and more is life, is it not? And you want to do something with it, you want to give it shape, direction, significance. Now, who is the 'you' that wants to do all this? Are you different from that which you seek to change?

'Are you suggesting that one should just go on drifting?'

When you want to direct, to shape life, your pattern can only be according to the past; or, being unable to shape it, your re-action is to drift. But the understanding of the totality of life brings about its own action, in which there is neither drifting nor the imposition of a pattern. This totality is to be understood from moment to moment. There must be the death of the past moment.

'But am I capable of understanding the totality of life?' he asked anxiously.

If you do not understand it, no one else can understand it for you. You cannot learn it from another.

'How shall I proceed?'

Through self-knowledge; for the totality, the whole treasure of life, lies within yourself.

'What do you mean by self-knowledge?'

It is to perceive the ways of your own mind; it is to learn about your cravings, your desires, your urges and pursuits, the hidden as well as the open. There is no learning where there is the accumulation of knowledge. With self-knowledge, the mind is free to be still. Only then is there the coming into being of that which is beyond the measure of the mind.

The married couple had been listening the whole time; they had been awaiting their turn, but never interrupted, and only now the husband spoke up.

'Our problem was that of jealousy, but after listening to what has already been said here, I think we may be capable of resolving it. Perhaps we have understood more deeply by quietly listening than we would have by asking questions.'

From Letters to the Schools Volume One, *1 December 1978*

To LEARN THE art of living one must have leisure. The word *leisure* is greatly misunderstood. Generally it means not to be occupied with the things we have to do such as earning a livelihood, going to the office, factory, and so on, and only when that is over is there leisure. During that so-called leisure you want to be amused, you want to relax, you want to do the things that you really like or that demand your highest capacity. Your earning a livelihood, whatever you do, is in opposition to so-called leisure. So there is always the strain, the tension and the escape from that tension, and leisure is when you have no strain. During that leisure you pick up a newspaper, open a novel, chatter, play, and so on. This is the actual fact. This is what is going on everywhere. Earning a livelihood is the denial of living.

So we come to the question—what is leisure? Leisure, as it is understood, is a respite from the pressure of livelihood. The pressure of earning a living, or any pressure imposed on us, we generally consider an absence of leisure, but there is a much greater pressure in us, conscious or unconscious, which is desire.

School is a place of leisure. It is only when you have leisure that you can learn. That is, learning can only take place when there is no pressure of any kind. When a snake or a danger confronts you, there is a kind of learning from the pressure of the fact of that danger. The learning under that pressure is the cultivation of memory that will help you to recognize future danger and so becomes a mechanical response.

Leisure implies a mind that is not occupied. It is only then that there is a state of learning. School is a place of learning and not merely a place for accumulating knowledge. This is really important to understand. As we said, knowledge is necessary and has its own limited place in life. Unfortunately this limitation has devoured all our lives and we have no space for learning. We are so occupied with our livelihood that it takes all the energy of the mechanism of thought, so that we are exhausted at the end of the day and need to be stimulated. We recover from this exhaustion through entertainment—religious or otherwise. This is the life of human beings. Human beings have created a society that demands all their time, all their energies, all their life. There is no leisure to learn and so their life becomes mechanical, almost meaningless. So we must be very clear in the understanding of the word *leisure*—a time, a period, when the mind is not occupied with anything whatsoever. It is the time of observation. It is only the unoccupied mind that can observe. A free observation is the movement of learning. This frees the mind from being mechanical.

So can the teacher, the educator, help the student to understand this whole business of earning a livelihood with all its pressure, the learning that helps you to acquire a job with all its fears and anxieties, and the looking on tomorrow with dread? Because he himself has understood the nature of leisure and pure observation, so that earning a livelihood does not become a torture, a great travail throughout life, can the teacher help the student to have a non-mechanical mind? It is the absolute responsibility of the teacher to cultivate the flowering of goodness in leisure. For this reason the schools exist. It is the responsibility of the teacher to create a new generation to change the social structure from its total preoccupation with earning a livelihood. Then teaching becomes a holy act.

From This Matter of Culture, *Chapter 7, with Young People*

WE HAVE BEEN discussing how essential it is to have love, and we saw that one cannot acquire or buy it; yet without love, all our plans for a perfect social order in which there is no exploitation, no regimentation, will have no meaning at all, and I think it is very important to understand this while we are young.

Wherever one goes in the world, it does not matter where, one finds that society is in a perpetual state of conflict. There are always the powerful, the rich, the well-to-do on the one hand, and the labourers on the other; and each one is enviously competing, each one wants a higher position, a bigger salary, more power, greater prestige. That is the state of the world, and so there is always war going on both within and without.

Now, if you and I want to bring about a complete revolution in the social order, the first thing we have to understand is this instinct for the acquisition of power. Most of us want power in one form or another. We see that through wealth and power we shall be able to travel, associate with important people, and become famous; or we dream of bringing about a perfect society. We think we shall achieve that which is good through power; but the very pursuit of power—power for ourselves, power for our country, power for an ideology—is evil, destructive, because it inevitably creates opposing powers, and so there is always conflict.

Is it not right, then, that education should help you as you grow up to perceive the importance of bringing about a world in which there is no conflict either within or without, a world in which you are not in conflict with your neighbour or with any group of people because the drive of ambition, which is the desire for position and power, has utterly ceased? And is it possible to create a society in which there will be no inward or outward conflict? Society is the relationship between you and me; and if our relationship is based on ambition, each one of us wanting to be more powerful than the other, then obviously we shall always be in conflict. So can this cause of conflict be removed? Can we all educate ourselves not to be competitive, not to compare ourselves with somebody else, not to want this or that position—in a word, not to be ambitious at all?

When you go outside the school with your parents, when you read the newspapers or talk to people, you must have noticed that almost everybody wants to bring about a change in the world. And have you not also noticed that these very people are always in conflict with each other over something or other—over ideas, property, race, caste, or religion? Your parents, your neighbours, the ministers and bureaucrats—are they not all ambitious, struggling for a better position, and therefore always in conflict with somebody? Surely it is only when all this competitiveness is removed that there will be a peaceful society in which all of us can live happily, creatively.

Now how is this to be done? Can regulation, legislation, or the training of your mind not to be ambitious, do away with ambition? Outwardly you may be trained not to be ambitious, socially you may cease to compete with others, but inwardly you will still be ambitious, will you not? And is it possible to sweep away completely this ambition, which is bringing so much misery to human beings? Probably you have not thought about it before, because nobody has talked to you like this; but now that somebody is talking to you about it, don't you want to find out if it is possible to live in this world richly, fully, happily, creatively, without the destructive drive of ambition, without competition? Don't you want to know how to live so that your life will not destroy another or cast a shadow across his path?

You see, we think this is a Utopian dream that can never be brought about in fact; but I am not talking about Utopia, that would be nonsense. Can you and I, who are simple, ordinary people, live creatively in this world without the drive of ambition, which shows itself in various ways as the desire for power, position? You will find the right answer when you love what you are doing. If you are an engineer merely because you must earn a livelihood, or because your father or society expects it of you, that is another form of compulsion; and compulsion in any form creates a contradiction, conflict. Whereas, if you really love to be an engineer, or a scientist or if you can plant a tree, or paint a picture, or write a poem, not to gain recognition but just because you love to do it, then you will find that you never compete with another. I think this is the real key: to love what you do.

But when you are young it is often very difficult to know what you love to do, because you want to do so many things. You want to be an engineer, a locomotive driver, an airplane pilot zooming along in the blue skies; or perhaps you want to be a famous orator or politician. You may want to be an artist, a chemist, a poet, or a carpenter. You may want to work with your head, or do something with your hands. Is any of these things what you really love to do, or is your interest in them merely a reaction to social pressures? How can you find out? And is not the true purpose of education to help you to find out, so that as you grow up you can begin to give your whole mind, heart, and body to that which you really love to do?

To find out what you love to do demands a great deal of intelligence; because if you are afraid of not being able to earn a livelihood, or of not fitting into this rotten society, then you will never find out. But if you are not frightened, if you refuse to be pushed into the groove of tradition by your parents, by your teachers, by the superficial demands of society, then there is a possibility of discovering what it is you really love to do. So to discover, there must be no fear of not surviving.

But most of us are afraid of not surviving. We say, 'What will happen to me if I don't do as my parents say, if I don't fit into this society?' Being frightened, we do as we are told, and in that there is no love, there is only contradiction; and this inner contradiction is one of the factors that bring about destructive ambition.

So it is a basic function of education to help you to find out what you really love to do, so that you can give your whole mind and heart to it, because that creates human dignity, that sweeps away mediocrity, the petty bourgeois mentality. That is why it is very important to have the right teachers, the right atmosphere so that you will grow up with the love that expresses itself in what you are doing. Without this love your examinations, your knowledge, your capacities, your position and possessions are just ashes, they have no meaning; without this love your actions are going to bring more wars, more hatred, more mischief and destruction.

All this may mean nothing to you, because outwardly you are still very young, but I hope it will mean something to your teachers—and also to you, somewhere inside.

From Letters to the Schools
Volume One, *15 December 1978*

EDUCATION IS NOT merely the teaching of various academic subjects, but the cultivation of total responsibility in the student. One does not realize as an educator that one is bringing into being a new generation. Most schools are only concerned with imparting knowledge. They are not at all concerned with the transformation of man and his daily life, and you—the educator in these schools—need to have this deep concern and the care of this total responsibility.

In what manner then can you help the student to feel this quality of love with all its excellence? If you do not feel this yourself profoundly, talking about responsibility is meaningless. Can you as an educator feel the truth of this?

Seeing the truth of it will bring about naturally this love and total responsibility. You have to ponder it, observe it daily in your life, in your relations with your wife, your friends, your students. And in your relationship with the students, you will talk about this from your heart, not pursue mere verbal clarity. The feeling for this reality is the greatest gift that man can have, and once it is burning in you, you will find the right word, right action, and correct behaviour. When you consider the student you will see that he comes to you totally unprepared for all this. He comes to you frightened, nervous, anxious to please, or on the defensive, conditioned by his parents and the society in which he has lived his few years. You have to see his background, you have to be concerned with what he actually is and not impose on him your own opinions, conclusions, and judgments. In considering what he is it will reveal what you are, and so you will find the student is you.

And now can you in the teaching of mathematics, physics, and so on—which he must know for that is the way of earning a livelihood—convey to the student that he is responsible for the whole of mankind? Though he may be working for his own career, his own way of life, it will not make his mind narrow. He will see the danger of specialization with all its limitations and strange brutality. You have to help him to see all this. The flowering of goodness does not lie in knowing mathematics and biology or in passing examinations and having a successful career. It exists outside these and when there is this flowering, career and other necessary activities are touched by its beauty. Now we lay emphasis on one and disregard the flowering entirely. In these schools we are trying to bring these two together, not artificially, not as a principle or pattern you are following, but because you see the absolute truth that these two must flow together for the regeneration of man.

Can you do this? Not because you all agree to do it after discussing and coming to a conclusion, but rather see with an inward eye the extraordinary gravity of this—see for yourself. Then what you say will have significance. Then you become a centre of light not lit by another. As you are all of humanity—which is an actuality not a verbal statement—you are utterly responsible for the future of man. Please do not consider this as a burden. If you do, that burden is a bundle of words without any reality. It is an illusion. This responsibility has its own gaiety, its own humour, its own movement without the weight of thought.

Saanen, 28 July 1979

Krishnamurti: If I may, I would like to suggest something. We have been talking about meditation, love, thought, and other things, but it seems to me that we are not talking about our daily life, our relationship with others, our relationship to the world, our relationship to the whole of humanity. And we seem to be wandering away from the central issue all the time, which is our daily life, the way we live, and whether we are at all aware of our daily turmoil, daily anxieties, daily insecurity, daily depressions, the constant demand of our daily existence. Shouldn't we be concerned with that? I am just asking whether we could not talk together as friends about our daily life, what we do, what we eat, what our relationships are, why we get so bored with our existence, why our minds are so mechanical, and so on. Could we talk about that? And restrict ourselves to that only.

Questioner: Yes.

K: What is our daily life? Not the escape into some fantasies, but getting up, exercising if you are inclined, eating, going off to the office, the factory, or some business or other, and our ambitions, fulfilments, our relationships with others, intimate or not intimate, sexual or not sexual, and so on. What is the central issue of our life? Is it money? Not the peripheral issues, not the superficial issues, but the deep demand. What is it that we demand, we ask? Is it that we want money? We need money. Is money the central issue? Or to have a position? To be secure, financially, psychologically; to be completely certain, unconfused? What is the main urge, demand, desire of our life?

Q: Joy of work.

K: Joy of work. Would you say that to the man who is turning the screw day after day, day after day, on a moving belt? Or to a man who has to go to the office every morning, and is told what to do every day of his life? Please face it. That is what we are asking: Is it money? Is it security? Is it lack of work? And having work, then there is the routine, the boredom of it, and the escape through entertainment, night-clubs, you follow? Anything away from our central existence. Because the world is in a horrible condition. You must know all this. So as fairly intelligent, serious, human beings, what is our relationship to all that? The moral deterioration, the intellectual dishonesty, the class prejudices, and so on. The mess that the politicians are making. The endless preparation for war. What is our relationship to all this?

Q: We are all part of it.

K: I quite agree. Do we know we are part of it? Aware that our *daily* life contributes to all this? And as it does, what shall we do? Take drugs? Get drunk? Join some community? Go off to a monastery? Or put on yellow, purple, bright colours? Would that solve all this? What shall we do? What is our daily life, of which society is made? The politicians are thoughtlessly using us for their own power, for their own position. So being aware of all this, what is our relationship to that, and what is our life, which obviously is contributing to that?

Q: We would like to change the way of living that we have now.

K: The way we are living now; we don't know how to change it. Therefore we accept it. Why is it that we can't change it?

Q: Perhaps we wait for someone else to tell us.

K: Are you waiting for some miracle to happen? Are we waiting for some authority to tell us what to do? The priest, the guru, the whole racket of that?

Now why can't we in our daily life change what we are doing? Let's come back: What is our daily life? I am asking if we are part of society, which is becoming more and more horrible, more and more intolerable, ugly, destructive, degenerating, and as a human being, is one also deteriorating?

Q: I think we don't see it.

K: Why? Don't we know our own daily life?

Q: Our daily life is a self-centred activity.

K: Our inner life, our life is self-centred activity. If that is so, and if that is contributing to the monstrous society in which we live, why can't we change that central activity, egotistic activity? Why can't we?

Q: We are unconscious of our own lives. Until we become conscious of everything that we are doing we can't change it.

K: I understand. That is what I am asking. Can we become conscious, aware of the activities of our daily life, of what we are doing?

Q: Being a mother, and having children, it is very difficult.

K: All right. Being a mother and having children, it is a very difficult life. Is that one of our problems? I am a mother. I have children, and are they growing up into monsters, like the rest of the world? Ugly, violent, self-centred, acquisitive, you know what we are. Do I want my children to be like that?

Q: Could we at least try to short-circuit the negation of our past conditioning, which we should know in its entirety by now, not fragmentarily, and think how in our everyday lives each one of us can put a sort of universal love into service, without any motives, to our fellow human beings.

Q: I would say it is not jobs in the big cities that are the problem, but I have this problem with my children; for me it seems that I have to wake up to the quality of my conditioning in relationship with my children and everything around me. This seems to be my problem, not the outside conditions.

K: What shall we do together?

Q: Can we look at fear?

K: We can look at fear. If you loved your children, they would not be sent off to schools in which they must be conditioned this way. Apparently it is not a problem to you. You talk about it, but it isn't a biting, demanding, urgent problem.

Q: Most people just go to work every day and there is no blending of their work and their recreation. But there could be learning all the time, and when the bell rings and you are free to leave you can still learn. You may adapt your job to your recreation, you can adapt your recreation to your job, but there is always a learning process going on. This doesn't seem to be happening at all. How many people go home and consider their jobs when they are not at their office? How many people go home and try to learn more about their lives whether they are at work or whether they are at home?

K: Having said that, where am I? Where are you? Are we still dealing with what might be, what should be, what ought to be, or are we facing the fact? You understand? Facing the fact.

Q: We are facing the fact there is a big separation between our work lives and our free time.

K: Do we face the fact that we are part of this society? We have contributed to it, our parents, our grandparents, and so on have contributed to this, and one is contributing. Is that a fact? Do I realize that?

Q: It is very clear that that is so.

K: Let us take that one point and work it out slowly. Do we realize, in the sense that we realize pain, realize a toothache, that we are contributing to it? Right? Do we?

Q: Yes, we do.

Q: Yes, we are contributing to it with eyes of our own past conditioning if we are still involved in it.

K: That's 'if', 'ought', 'might'. . . . Can't you face the fact? When we say, 'I am part of that society', what do we mean by that?. . . Can't we think together about this one thing: that is, we human beings have created this society, not gods, not angels, nobody but human beings have created this terrible, violent, destructive society. And we are part of that. When we say we are part of it, what do we mean by that word *part?*

Q: Isn't the approach you are taking already setting up a division between me and society? In other words, is there such a thing as society? When you set up this monstrous, horrible society, it is an abstraction that is different from the people in this room.

K: No, I am saying that society is not out there; society is here.

Q: Right here?

K: Yes, right here.

Q: Well then can't we all work together and lose our past conditioning of these words that you have been saying to us for all of these years, and begin to act in some form or other that is new and creative?

K: We can't work together. That is a fact. We can't think together, and we don't seem to be able to do anything together, unless we are forced; unless there is a tremendous crisis, like war; then we all come together. If there is an earthquake we are all involved in it. But remove the earthquakes, the great crises of war, and we are back to our separative little selves, fighting each other. This is so obvious.

    Can we just look at this for a minute? When we say we are part of that society, is it an idea, or an actuality? By idea, I mean a concept, a picture, a conclusion. Or is it a fact, like having a toothache?

Q: I am that society.

K: I am that society. Then what is happening out there to which I am contributing? Am I seeking my own security, my own experiences, involved in my own problems, concerned with my own ambitions? So each one is striving for himself as society exists now. And probably that has been the historical process from the beginning: each one struggling for himself, and therefore each one opposed to another. Now, do we realize that?

Q: Yes.

Q: We don't know what to do . . .

K: We'll find out what to do, but let us start from that which is very near, and then we can go on. We are talking about our daily life. And our daily life is not only part of society, but also we are encouraging this society by our activities. Then what shall I, as a human being, being part of this society, do? What is my responsibility? Take drugs? Grow a beard? Run off? What is my responsibility?

Q: To do something about it.

K: I can only do something about it when I am clear in myself.

Q: Is it not astonishing that if we are clear and logical about it, we can be excluded from the society?

K: All right. So let's find out how to be clear in oneself. How to be certain about things. Let's find out if one can have security. Both psychological and physical. So how does a mind that is confused, as most people's are, how is that confusion to be wiped away so that there is clarity? If there is clarity, from there I can act. Right?

Q: Yes.

K: Now how am I to have clarity about politics, about work, about my relationship with my wife, husband, and all the rest of it—relationship to the world? How am I to be clear when I am so confused? The gurus say one thing, the priests say something else, the economists and the philosophers say something else—you follow? The analysts say something about primordial pain, or whatever it is. So they are all shouting, writing, explaining. And I am caught in that and I get more and more confused. I don't know what to do to be clear, who is right, who is wrong. That is our position, isn't it?

Q: Yes.

K: So I say to myself, I am confused. That confusion has been caused by all these people, each one saying different things. So I am confused. So I say I am not going to listen to any of you; I am going to see why I am confused. Let's start from there.

From Letters to the Schools
Volume Two, *15 November 1983*

BY WATCHING PERHAPS you learn more than from books. Books are necessary to learn a subject, whether it be mathematics, geography, history, physics, or chemistry. The books have printed on a page the accumulated knowledge of scientists, of philosophers, of archaeologists, and so on. This accumulated knowledge that one learns in school and then through college or university, if one is lucky enough to go to university, has been gathered through the ages, from the very ancient of days. There is great accumulated knowledge from India, from ancient Egypt, Mesopotamia, the Greeks, the Romans, and of course the Persians. In the Western world as well as in the Eastern world this knowledge is necessary to have a career, to do any job, whether mechanical or theoretical, practical or something that you have to think out, invent. This knowledge has brought about a great deal of technology, especially within this century. There is the knowledge of the so-called sacred books, the Vedas, the Upanishads, the Bible, the Koran, and the Hebrew scriptures. So there are the religious books and pragmatic books, books that will help you to have knowledge, to act skilfully, whether you are an engineer, a biologist, or a carpenter.

Most of us in any school, and particularly in these schools, gather knowledge, information, and that is what schools have existed for so far: to gather a great deal of information about the world outside, about the heavens, why the sea is salty, why the trees grow, about human beings, their anatomy, the structure of the brain, and so on. And also about the world around you, nature, the social environment, economics, and so much else. Such knowledge is absolutely necessary, but knowledge is always limited. However much it may evolve, the gathering of knowledge is always limited. Learning is part of acquiring this knowledge of various subjects so that you can have a career, a job that might please you, or one that circumstances, social demands may have forced you to accept, though you may not like very much to do that kind of work.

You learn a great deal by watching, watching the things about you, watching the birds, the trees, watching the heavens, the stars, the constellation of Orion, the Dipper, the Evening Star. You learn just by watching not only the things around you, but also by watching people, how they walk, their gestures, the words they use, how they are dressed. You watch not only that which is outside but also yourself, why you think this or that, your behaviour, the conduct of your daily life, why parents want you to do one thing or another. You are watching, not resisting. If you resist you don't learn. Or if you come to some kind of conclusion, some opinion you think is right and hold on to that, then naturally you will never learn. Freedom is necessary to learn, and curiosity, a sense of wanting to know why you or others behave in a certain way, why people are angry, why you get annoyed.

Learning is extraordinarily important because learning is endless. Learning why human beings kill each other for instance. Of course there are explanations in books, all the psychological reasons why human beings behave in their own particular manner, why human beings are violent. All this has been explained in books of various kinds by eminent authors, psychologists, and so on. But what you read is not what you are. What you are, how you behave, why you get angry, envious, why you get depressed, if you watch yourself you learn much more than from a book that tells you what you are. But you see it is easier to read a book about yourself than to watch yourself. The brain is accustomed to gather information from all external actions and reactions. Don't you find it much more comforting to be directed, for others to tell you what you should do? Your parents, especially in the East, tell you whom you should marry and arrange the marriage, tell you what your career should be. So the brain accepts the easy way and the easy way is not always the right way. I wonder if you have noticed that nobody loves their work any more, except perhaps a few scientists, artists, archaeologists. But the ordinary, average man seldom loves what he is doing. He is compelled by society, by his parents, or by the urge to have more money. So learn by watching very, very carefully the external world, the world outside you, and the inner world; that is, the world of yourself.

There appear to be two ways of learning: One is acquiring a great deal of knowledge, first through study and then by acting from that knowledge. That is what most of us do. The second is to act, to do something and learn through doing, and that also becomes the accumulation of knowledge. Really both are the same: learning from a book or acquiring knowledge through action. Both are based upon knowledge, experience, and as we have said, experience and knowledge are always limited.

So both the educator and the student should find out what learning actually is. For example you learn from a guru if he is at all the right kind, a sane guru, not the moneymaking guru, not one of those who want to be famous and trot off to different countries to gather a fortune through their rather unbalanced theories. Find out what it is to learn. Today learning is becoming more and more a form of entertainment. In some Western schools when they have passed high school, secondary school, the students do not even know how to read and write. And when you do know how to read and write and learn various subjects you are all such mediocre people. Do you know what the word *mediocrity* means? The root meaning is to go half way up the hill, never reaching the top. That is mediocrity: never demanding the excellent, the very highest thing of yourself. And learning is infinite, it really has no end. So from whom are you learning? From the books? From the educator? And perhaps, if your mind is bright, by watching? So far it appears you are learning from the outside: learning, accumulating knowledge and from that knowledge acting, establishing your career, and so on. If you are learning from yourself—or rather if you are learning by watching yourself, your prejudices, your definite conclusions, your beliefs—if you are watching the subtleties of your thought, your vulgarity, your sensitivity, then you become yourself the teacher and the taught. Then you do not depend inwardly on anybody, not on any book, not on the specialist—though of course if you are ill and have some sort of disease you have to go to a specialist; that is natural, that is necessary. But to depend on somebody, however excellent he may be, prevents you from learning about yourself and what you are. And it is very, very important to learn what you are because what you are brings about this society that is so corrupt, immoral, where there is such enormous spreading of violence, that is so aggressive, each one seeking his own particular success, his own form of fulfilment. Learn what you are not through another but by watching yourself, not condemning, not saying, 'This is all right, I am that, I can't change', and carrying on. When you watch yourself without any form of reaction, resistance, then that very watching acts; like a flame it burns away the stupidities, the illusions that one has.

So learning becomes important. A brain that ceases to learn becomes mechanical. It is like an animal tied to a stick; it can move only according to the length of the rope, the tether that is tied to the stick. Most of us are tied to a peculiar stake of our own, an invisible stake and rope. You keep wandering within the dimensions of that rope and it is very limited. It is like a man who is thinking about himself all day, about his problems, his desires, his pleasures, and what he would like to do. You know this constant occupation with oneself. It is very, very limited. And that very limitation breeds various forms of conflict and unhappiness.

The great poets, painters, composers are never satisfied with what they have done. They are always learning. It isn't that after you have passed your exams and gone to work you stop learning. There is a great strength and vitality in learning, especially about yourself. Learn, watch, so that there is no spot that is not uncovered, looked at in yourself. This really is to be free from your own particular conditioning. The world is divided through its conditioning: you as an Indian, you as an American, you as British, Russian, Chinese, and so on. Out of this conditioning there are wars, the killing of thousands of people, unhappiness, and brutality.

So both the educator and the educated are learning in the deeper sense of that word. When both are learning, there is no educator or one to be educated. There is only learning. Learning frees the brain and thought of prestige, position, status.

Learning brings about equality among human beings.

From Beginnings of Learning, *Chapter 13, Dialogue at Brockwood Park School, 17 June 1973*

Krishnamurti: The other day we were talking about sanity and mediocrity, what those words mean. We were asking whether living in this place as a community we are mediocre. And we also asked whether we are sane totally, that is bodily, mentally, emotionally. Are we balanced and healthy? All that is implied in the words *sane, whole.* Are we educating each other to be mediocre, to be slightly insane, slightly off balance?

The world is quite insane, unhealthy, corrupt. Are we bringing about that same imbalance, insanity, and corruption in our education here? This is a very serious question. Can we find out the truth of it?—not what we think we should be in terms of sanity, but actually discover for ourselves if we are educating each other to be really sane and not mediocre.

Questioner: Many of us will have a job to which we have to go every day, many people will get married and have children—those are things that are going to happen.

K: What is your place in this world as a human being who is supposed to be educated, who has got to earn a livelihood, where you may, or may not marry, have the responsibility of children, a house and mortgage, and may be trapped in that for the rest of your life?

Q: Perhaps we are hoping somebody will look after us.

K: That means you must be capable of doing something. You can't just say, 'Please look after me'—nobody is going to do it. Don't be depressed by it. Just look at it, be familiar with it, know all the tricks people are playing on each other. The politicians will never bring the world together, on the contrary; there may be no actual war but there is an economic war going on. If you are a scientist you are a slave to the government. All governments are more or less corrupt, some more, some less, but all are corrupt. So look at all this without getting depressed and saying, 'What am I going to do, how am I going to face this? I haven't the capacity.' You will have the capacity; when you know how to look you will have tremendous capacity.

So what is your place in all this? If you see the whole, then you can ask that question, but if you merely say to yourself, 'What am I going to do?' without seeing the whole, then you are caught, then there is no answer to it.

Q: Surely the first thing is for us to discuss these things openly. But I think people are a little frightened to discuss freely. Perhaps the thing they really care about will be threatened.

K: Are you frightened?

Q: If I say what I want is a fast car, then perhaps somebody will question that.

K: It must be questioned. I get letters questioning me all the time; I have been challenged since my childhood.

Q: Sir, there is something that always bothers me when these things are discussed. It is said we live in a highly mechanized industrial society and if some of us can opt out of it, it is because there are other people who do go to the office and work and become mechanical.

K: Of course.

Q: We couldn't opt out of it without those people fulfilling their mechanical, miserable existence.

K: No. How to live in this world without belonging to it, that is the question. How to live in this insanity and yet be sane?

Q: Are you saying that the man who goes to the office and leads an apparently mechanical life could do all that and yet be a different sort of human being? In other words, it isn't necessarily the system . . .

K: This system, whatever it is, is making the mind mechanical.

Q: But does it have to make the mind mechanical?

K: It is happening.

Q: All young people are faced with growing up, they see they may have to take a job that entails that. Can there be another response to it?

K: My question is: How to live in this insane world sanely? Though I may have to go to an office and earn a livelihood, there must be a different heart, a different mind. Is this different mind, this different heart happening here in this place? Or are we just treading the mill and getting thrown out into this monstrous world?

Q1: There is no need any more to have a nine-to-five, six-day-a-week job because of automation. What is happening is that this age is now giving us the extra time to attend to our other side.

Q2: But we were saying we want leisure, and we don't know how to use leisure.

Q3: There is nothing wrong, surely, in earning a livelihood?

K: I never said it's wrong to earn a livelihood; one has to earn a livelihood. I earn my livelihood by talking to people in many places. I have been doing it for fifty years and I am doing what I love to do. What I am doing is really what I think is right, is true; it is the way of living for me—not imposed on me by somebody—and that is my way of earning a livelihood.

Q: I just want to say that you are able to do that because there are people who fly the airplanes.

K: Of course, I know that; without them I couldn't travel. But if there were no airplanes I would remain in one place, in the village where I was born and I would still be doing the same thing there.

Q: Yes, but in this highly mechanized society, where profit is the motive, this is the way things are organized.

K: No, other people do the dirty work, and I do the clean work.

Q: So one tries to do the clean work?

K: It comes to that.

Q: But apart from earning a living, we have to begin to realize that to live sanely and yet earn a living in this world, there has to be an inner revolution.

K: I am putting the same question differently. How am I to live sanely in this world that is insane? It doesn't mean I am not going to earn a livelihood, that I am not going to marry, that I am not going to take responsibilities. To live in this insane world sanely, I must reject that world and a revolution in me must come about so that I become sane and operate sanely. That's my whole point.

Q: Because I've been brought up insanely I have to question everything.

K: That's what education is. You have been sent here, or you came here, contaminated by an insane world. Don't fool yourself, you have been conditioned by that insane world, shaped by past generations—including your parents—and you come here and you have to uncondition yourself, you have to undergo a tremendous change. Does that change take place? Or are we just saying: 'Well, we are doing a bit of good work here and there, day after day', and by the time you leave in two or four years' time, off you go with a little patchwork done?

Q: There seems to be a conflict between what we want to do, what we desire to do, and what is necessary.

K: What is it you desire to do? I want to be an engineer because I see it brings in a great deal of money, or this or that. Can I rely on that desire? Can I rely on my instincts that have been so twisted? Can I rely on my thoughts? What have I to rely on? So education is to create an intelligence that is not mere instinct or desire or some petty demand, but an intelligence that will function in this world.

Is our education at Brockwood helping you to be intelligent? I mean by that word: to be very sensitive, not to your own desires, to your own demands, but to be sensitive to the world, to what is going on in the world. Surely education is not merely to give you knowledge, but also to give you the capacity to look at the world objectively, to see what is happening—the wars, the destruction, the violence, the brutality. The function of education is to find out how to live differently, not merely to pass exams, to get a degree, become qualified in certain ways. It is to help you to face the world in a totally different, intelligent way, knowing you have to earn a livelihood, knowing all the responsibilities, the miseries of it all. My question is: Is this being done here? Is the educator getting educated as well as the student?

Q: Your question is also my question. I ask whether this education is happening here.

K: You are asking whether such education is taking place here at Brockwood to help you to become so intelligent, so aware that you can meet this insanity? If not, whose fault is it?

Q: What is the basis that makes this education possible?

K: Look, why are you being educated?

Q: I really don't know.

K: Therefore you have to find out what education means, mustn't you? What is education? Giving you information, knowledge about various subjects and so on, a good academic training? That has to be, hasn't it? Millions of people are being turned out by the universities and colleges.

Q: They give you the tools to live with.

K: But what are the hands that are going to use them? They are the same hands that have produced this world, the wars and all the rest of it.

Q: Which means the tools are there but if there is no inner, psychological revolution you will use those tools in the same old way and keep the rottenness going. That's what my question is about.

K: If this revolution does not take place here, then why doesn't it? And if it does, is it actually affecting the mind, or is it still an idea and not an actuality, like having to eat three meals a day. That is an actuality, somebody has to cook, that's not an idea.

So I am asking you, is this kind of education we are talking about taking place here? And if it is, let us find out how to vitalize it, give life to it. If it is not, let's find out why.

Q: It doesn't seem to be happening in the whole school.

K: Why not? It may be happening with a few individuals here and there—why isn't it happening with all of us?

Q: I feel it's like a seed that wants to germinate but the topsoil is too heavy.

K: Have you seen grass growing through cement?

Q1: Well, this is a weak seed, you see. (Laughter.)

Q2: But do we realize that we are mediocre and do we want to get out of it?—that's the point.

K: I am asking you: Are you mediocre? I am not using that word in any derogatory sense—I am using the word *mediocre* as it is described in the dictionary. You are bound to be middle class if you merely pursue your own little activities instead of seeing the whole—the whole world and your particular little place in the whole, not the other way round. People don't see the whole, they are pursuing their little desires, their little pleasures, their little vanities and brutalities, but if they saw the whole and understood their place in it, their relationship to the whole would be totally different.

You, living at Brockwood as a student in a small community, in relationship with your teachers and your fellow students, do you see the whole of what is going on in the world? That is the first thing. To see it objectively, not emotionally, not with prejudice, not with a bias, but just look at it. The various governments will not solve this problem, no politician is interested in this. They want more or less to maintain the status quo, with a little alteration here and there. They don't want the unity of man, they want the unity of England. But even there the different political parties don't say, 'Let's all join together and find out what is best for man.'

Q: But you are not saying it's not possible?

K: They are not doing it.

Q: Are we?

K: We are observing, we are first looking at the world. And when you see the whole thing, what is your desire in relation to the whole? If you don't see the whole and merely pursue your particular instinct or tendency or desire, that is the essence of mediocrity, that's what is happening in the world.

You see, in the old days the really serious people said, 'We will have nothing to do with the world, we will become monks, we will become preachers, we will live without property, without marriage, without position in society. We are teachers, we will go round the villages and the country, people will feed us, we will teach them morality, we will teach them how to be good, not to hate each other.' That used to happen, but we can't do that any more. In India one still can. You can go from the north to the south and from east to west begging. Put on a certain robe and they will feed you and clothe you because that is part of the tradition of India. But even that is beginning to fade, for there are so many charlatans.

So we have to earn a livelihood, we have to live in this world a life that is intelligent, sane, not mechanical—that is the point. And education is to help us to be sane, non-mechanical, and intelligent. I keep repeating this. Now how do we, you and I, discuss this thing and find out first what we actually are and see if that can be totally changed? So first look at yourself, don't avoid it, don't say, 'How terrible, how ugly.' Just observe whether you have got all the tendencies of the insanity that has produced this ugly world. And if you observe your own particular quirks, find out how to change. Let's talk about it, that is relationship, that is friendship, that is affection, that is love. Talk about it and say, 'Look, I am greedy, I feel terribly silly.' Can that be changed radically? That is part of our education.

Q: It's when I feel insecure that I become silly.

K: Of course. But are you sure? Don't theorize about it. Are you seeking security?—in somebody, in a profession, in some quality, or in an idea?

Q: One needs security.

K: You see how you defend it? First find out if you are seeking security; don't say one needs it. Then we will see whether it is needed or not, but first see if you are seeking security. Of course you are! Have you understood the meaning and the implications of that word *depending?*—depending on money, depending on people, on ideas, all coming from outside. To depend on some belief, or on the image you have about yourself, that you are a great man, that you have this or that, you know all this nonsense that goes on. So you have to understand what the implications of that word are and whether you are caught in those things. If you see you depend on somebody for your security then you begin to question, then you begin to learn. You begin to learn what is implied in dependency, in attachment. In security, fear and pleasure are involved. When there is no security you feel lost, you feel lonely; and when you feel lonely you escape—through drink, women, or whatever you do. You act neurotically because you haven't really solved this problem.

So find out, learn what the meaning, the significance, and the implications of that word are in actuality, not in theory. Learn:

that is part of our education. I depend on certain people. I depend on them for my security, for my safety, for my money, for my pleasure. Therefore if they do something that upsets me I get frightened, irritated, angry, jealous, frustrated, and then I rush off and put *my* claws into somebody else. The same problem goes on all the time. So I say to myself, let me first understand what this means. I must have money, I must have food, clothes, and shelter, those are normal things. But when money is involved the whole cycle begins. So I have to learn and know about the whole thing; not after I have committed myself, then it is too late. I commit myself by getting married to somebody and then I am caught, then I am dependent, then the battle begins, wanting to be free yet being caught by responsibility, by the mortgage.

Here is a problem: This boy says, 'I must have security.' I answered: Before you say 'I must', find out what it means, learn about it.

Q: I must have food and clothes and a house.

K: Yes, go on.

Q: To have that I need to earn enough money.

K: So you do whatever you can. Then what happens?

Q: To earn this money I depend on someone . . .

K: You depend on society, on your patron, on your employer. He chases you around, he is brutal, and you put up with it because you depend on him. That is what is happening right round the world. Please look at it first, as you look at a map. You say, 'I have to earn a livelihood. I know in earning a livelihood I am dependent on society as it exists. It demands so many hours a day for five or six days a week and if I don't earn a livelihood I have nothing. That's one thing. And I also depend inwardly on my wife or a priest or a counsellor.' Do you understand?

Q: So knowing all that I won't marry. I see the dependency, all the trouble that will come.

K: You are not learning. Don't say you won't marry, see what the problem is first. I need food, clothes, and shelter, those are primary needs and for those I depend on society as it is, whether it is Communist or Capitalist. I know that and I am going to look in other directions; I need security emotionally, that means dependence on somebody, on my wife, friends, neighbours, it doesn't matter who it is. And when I depend on somebody, fear always exists. I am learning, I am not saying what to do yet. I depend on you, you are my brother, my wife, my husband, and the moment you go away I am lost, I am frightened—I do neurotic things. I see dependence on people leads to that.

Also I ask: Do I depend on ideas? On a belief that there is a God—or not—that we must have universal brotherhood, whatever it is; that is another dependence. And you come along and say, 'What rubbish this is, you are living in a world of illusion.' So I get shaken and I say, 'What am I to do?' Then instead of learning about it I join some other cult. Do you see all this? Do you discover that in yourself you are insufficient and therefore you are dependent? Then you seek sufficiency in yourself: 'I am all right, I have found God, what I believe is true, my experience is the real thing.' So you ask: 'What is there that is so completely secure that it is never disturbed?'

Q: I don't see the dependency on the two things you were talking about . . .

K: We are asking what the implications of wanting security are. We're looking at the map of security. It shows that I depend on food, clothes, and shelter by working in a society that is corrupt—and I see what depending on people does. I am not saying this should be or that should not be. The map says: look, this road leads to fear, pleasure, anger, fulfilment, frustration, and neurosis. And it also says: look at the world of ideas. Depending on ideas is the most flimsy form of security, they are only words, which have become a reality as an image; you live on an image. And that map says: be self-sufficient. So I depend on myself, I must have confidence in myself. What is yourself? You are the result of all this. So the map has shown you all these things and you ask now, 'Where is there complete security—including a job and all the rest of it?' Where will you find it?

Q: You find it when you have no fears.

K: You haven't understood what I am saying. Put a map of this in front of you. Look at it all: physical security, emotional security, intellectual security, and security in your own thoughts, in your own feelings, in your self-confidence. You say, how flimsy all this is. Looking at it all and seeing the flimsiness, the invalidity, the lack of reality behind it, where is security then? It is learning about this which brings intelligence. So in intelligence there is security. Have you understood it?

Q: Can one live without security?

K: You haven't learned to look first. You have learned to look through your particular image; that image has given you the feeling of security. So first learn to look at the map, put aside the image of what you think is security—that you must have it—and just look. What are the implications of wanting security? When you find there is no security in anything that you have sought, that there is no security in death, no security in living, when you see all that, then the very seeing of the fact that there is no security in the things in which one had sought it, is intelligence. That intelligence gives you complete security.

So learning is the beginning of security. The act of learning is intelligence, and in learning there is tremendous security. Are you learning here?

Q: In the family they say one must manage to earn a living, have a certain amount of knowledge. There is this idea about security, this basic necessity.

K: That's quite right. Your family, the tradition says you must have physical security, you must have a job, you must have knowledge, a technique, you must specialize, you must be this, you must be that, in order to have that security.

Q: It's an idea.

K: I need money, that's not an idea—everything else is an idea. The physical continuity in security is the real thing; everything else has no reality. And to see that is intelligence. In that intelligence there is the most complete security; I can live anywhere, in the Communist world or in a Capitalist world.

Do you remember we said the other day that meditation is to observe? That is the beginning of meditation. You cannot observe this map if you have the slightest distortion in your mind, if your mind is distorted by prejudice, by fear. To look at this map is to look without prejudice. So learn in meditation what it is to be free of prejudice; that is part of meditation, not just sitting cross-legged in some place. It makes you tremendously responsible, not only for yourself and your relationship but for everything else, the garden, the trees, the people around you—everything becomes tremendously important.

To be serious is also to have fun. You can't be serious without having fun. We talked the other day about yoga, didn't we? I showed you some breathing exercises. You must do it all with fun, enjoy things—you follow?

Q: There are certain things like learning that I don't think it's possible to discuss with a sense of fun.

K: Oh yes! It is. Look, learning is fun. To see new things is great fun; it gives you tremendous energy if you make a great discovery for yourself—not if someone else discovers it and tells you about it, then it's second-hand. When you are learning it is fun to see something totally new, like discovering a new insect, a new species. To discover how my mind is working, to see all the nuances, the subtleties, to learn about it is fun.

From Questions and Answers, *Saanen, 24 July 1980*

Right Living

Questioner: I work as a teacher and I am in constant conflict with the system of the school and the pattern of society. Must I give up all work? What is the right way to earn a living? Is there a way of living that does not perpetuate conflict?

Krishnamurti: This is a rather complex question and we will go into it step by step.

What is a teacher? Either a teacher gives information about history, physics, biology, and so on, or he himself is learning together with the pupil about himself. This is a process of understanding the whole movement of life. If I am a teacher, not of biology or physics, but of psychology, then will the pupil understand me or will my pointing out help him to understand himself?

We must be very careful and clear as to what we mean by a teacher. Is there a teacher of psychology at all? Or are there only teachers of facts? Is there a teacher who will help you to understand yourself? The questioner asks: I am a teacher. I have to struggle not only with the established system of schools and education, but also my own life is a constant battle with myself. And must I give up all this? Then what shall I do if I give up all that? He is asking not only what right teaching is but he also wants to find out what right living is.

What is right living? As society exists now, there is no right way of living. You have to earn a livelihood, you marry, you have children, you become responsible for them, and so you accept the life of an engineer or a professor. As society exists can there be a right way of living? Or is the search for a right way of living merely a search for Utopia, a wish for something more? What is one to do in a society that is corrupt, that has such contradictions in itself, in which there is so much injustice—for that is the society in which we live? And not only as a teacher in a school, I am asking myself: What shall I do?

Is it possible to live in this society, not only to have a right means of livelihood, but also to live without conflict? Is it possible to earn a livelihood righteously and also to end all conflict within one-self? Now, are these two separate things: earning a living rightly and not having conflict in oneself? Are these two in separate, water-tight compartments? Or do they go together? To live a life without any conflict requires a great deal of understanding of oneself and therefore great intelligence—not the clever intelligence of the intellect—but the capacity to observe, to see objectively what is happening, both outwardly and inwardly and to know that there is no difference between the outer and the inner. It is like a tide that goes out and comes in. To live in this society, which we have created, without any conflict in myself and at the same time to have a right livelihood—is it possible? On which shall I lay emphasis—on right livelihood or on right living, that is, on finding out how to live a life without any conflict? Which comes first? Do not just let me talk and you listen, agreeing or disagreeing, saying, 'It is not practical. It is not like this, it is not like that'—because it is your problem. We are asking each other: Is there a way of living that will naturally bring about a right livelihood and at the same time enable us to live without a single shadow of conflict?

People have said that you cannot live that way except in a monastery, as a monk; because you have renounced the world and all its misery and are committed to the service of God, because you have given your life over to an idea, or a person, an image or symbol, you expect to be looked after. But very few believe any more in monasteries, or in saying, 'I will surrender myself.' If they do surrender themselves it will be surrendering to the image they have created about another, or that they have projected.

It is possible to live a life without a single shadow of conflict only when you have understood the whole significance of living, which is relationship and action. What is right action in *all* circumstances? Is there such a thing? Is there a right action that is absolute, not relative? Life is action, movement, talking, acquiring knowledge, and also relationship with another however deep or superficial. You have to find right relationship if you want to find a right action that is absolute.

What is your present relationship with another—not the romantic, imaginative, flowery, and superficial thing that disappears in a few minutes—but actually what is your relationship with another? What is your relationship with a particular person?—perhaps intimate, involving sex, involving dependence on each other, possessing each other and therefore arousing jealousy and antagonism. The man or the woman goes off to the office, or to do some kind of physical work, where he or she is ambitious, greedy, competitive, aggressive to succeed; he or she comes back home and becomes a tame, friendly, perhaps affectionate husband or wife. That is the actual daily relationship. Nobody can deny that. And we are asking: Is that right relationship? We say no, certainly not, it would be absurd to say that that is right relationship. We say that, but continue in the same way. We say that that is wrong but we do not seem to be able to understand what right relationship is—except according to the pattern set by ourselves, by society.

We may want it, we may wish for it, long for it, but longing and wishing do not bring it about. We have to go into it seriously to find out.

Relationship is generally sensuous—begin with that—then from sensuality there is companionship, a sense of dependence on each other; then there is the creating of a family, which increases dependence on each other. When there is uncertainty in that dependence, the pot boils over. To find right relationship one has to inquire into this great dependence on each other. Psychologically why are we so dependent in our relationships with each other? Is it that we are desperately lonely? Is it that we do not trust anybody—even our own husband or wife? On the other hand, dependence gives a sense of security, a protection against this vast world of terror. We say, 'I love you.' In that love there is always the sense of possessing and being possessed. And when that situation is threatened there arises all the conflict. That is our present relationship with each other, intimate or otherwise. We create an image about each other and cling to that image.

The moment you are tied to another person, or tied to an idea or concept, corruption has begun. That is the thing to realize and we do not want to realize it. So can we live together without being tied, without being dependent on each other psychologically? Unless you find this out you will always live in conflict, because life is relationship. Now, can we objectively, without any motive, observe the consequences of attachment and let them go immediately? Attachment is not the opposite of detachment. I am attached and I struggle to be detached; which is, I create the opposite. The moment I have created the opposite, conflict comes into being. But there is no opposite; there is only what I have, which is attachment. There is only the fact of attachment—in which I see all the consequences of attachment in which there is no love—not the pursuit of detachment. The brain has been conditioned, educated, trained, to observe what is and to create its opposite: 'I am violent but I must not be violent'—therefore there is conflict. But when I observe only violence, the nature of it—not analyse but observe—then the conflict of the opposite is totally eliminated. If one wants to live without conflict, only deal with 'what is', everything else is not. And when one lives that way—and it is possible to live that way—

completely to remain with 'what is', then 'what is' withers away.
Experiment with it.

When you really understand the nature of relationship,
which only exists when there is no attachment, when there is no
image about the other, then there is real communion with each
other.

Right action means precise, accurate action, not based on
motive; it is action that is not directed or committed. The understanding of right action, right relationship, brings about intelligence.
Not the intelligence of the intellect, but that profound intelligence
that is not yours or mine. That intelligence will dictate what you will
do to earn a livelihood; when there is that intelligence you may be
a gardener, a cook, it does not matter. Without that intelligence
your livelihood will be dictated by circumstance.

There is a way of living in which there is no conflict; because there is no conflict there is intelligence, which will show the
right way of living.

From Krishnamurti to Himself, *Brockwood Park, 30 May 1983*

IT HAS BEEN raining here every day for over a month. When you come from a climate like California where the rains stopped over a month ago, where the green fields were drying up and turning brown and the sun was very hot (it was over ninety degrees and would get hotter still, though they say it is going to be a mild summer)—when you come from that climate it is rather startling and surprising to see the green grass, the marvellous green trees, and the copper beeches, which are a spreading, light brown, becoming gradually darker and darker. To see them now among the green trees is a delight. They are going to be very dark as the summer comes on. And this earth is very beautiful. Earth, whether it is desert or filled with orchards and green, bright fields, is always beautiful.

To go for a walk in the fields with the cattle and the young lambs, and in the woods with the song of birds, without a single thought in your mind, only watching the earth, the trees, the sheep and hearing the cuckoo calling and the wood pigeons; to walk without any emotion, any sentiment, to watch the trees and all the earth—when you so watch, you learn your own thinking, are aware of your own reactions, and do not allow a single thought to escape you without understanding why it came, what was the cause of it. If you are watchful, never letting a thought go by, then the brain becomes very quiet. Then you watch in great silence and that silence has immense depth, a lasting incorruptible beauty.

The boy was good at games, really quite good. He was also good at his studies; he was serious. So one day he came to his teacher and said, 'Sir, could I have a talk with you?' The educator said, 'Yes, we can have a talk; let us go out for a walk.' So they had a dialogue. It was a conversation between the teacher and the taught, a conversation in which there was some respect on both sides, and as the educator was also serious, the conversation was pleasant, friendly, and they had forgotten that he was a teacher with a student; the rank was forgotten, the importance of one who knows, the authority, and the other who is curious.

'Sir, I wonder if you know what all this is about, why I am getting an education, what part will it play when I grow up, what role have I in this world, why do I have to study, why do I have to marry, and what is my future? Of course I realize I have to study and pass some sort of exams and I hope I will be able to pass them. I will probably live for some years, perhaps fifty, sixty or more, and in all those years to come what will be my life and the life of those people around me? What am I going to be and what is the point of these long hours over books and hearing the teachers? There might be a devastating war; we might all be killed. If death is all that lies ahead, then what is the point of all this education? Please, I am asking these questions quite seriously because I have heard the other teachers and you too pointing out many of these things.'

'I would like to take one question at a time. You have asked many questions, you have put several problems before me, so first let us look at perhaps the most important question: What is the future of mankind and of yourself? As you know, your parents are fairly well off and of course they want to help you in any way they can. Perhaps if you get married they might give you a house, buy a house with all the things necessary in it, and you might have a nice wife—might. So what is it you are going to be? The usual mediocre person? Get a job, settle down with all the problems around you and in you—is that your future? Of course a war may come, but it may not happen; let us hope it does not happen. Let us hope man may come to realize that wars of any kind will never solve any human problem. Men may improve, they may invent better airplanes and so on, but wars have never solved human problems and they never will. So let us forget for the moment that all of us might be destroyed through the craziness of super powers, through the craziness of terrorists or some demagogue in some country wanting to destroy his invented enemies. Let us forget all that for the moment. Let us consider what is your future, knowing that you are part of the rest of the world. What is your future? As I asked—to be a mediocre person? Mediocrity means to go half way up the hill, half way in anything, never going to the very top of the mountain or demanding all your energy, your capacity, never demanding excellence.

'Of course you must realize also that there will be all the pressures from outside—pressures to do this, all the various narrow religious sectarian pressures and propaganda. Propaganda can never tell the truth; truth can never be propagated. So I hope you realize the pressure on you—pressure from your parents, from your society, from the tradition to be a scientist, to be a philosopher, to be a physicist, a man who undertakes research in any field; or to be a business man. Realizing all this, which you must do at your age, what way will you go? We have been talking about all these things for many terms, and probably, if one may point out, you have applied your mind to all this. So as we have some time together to go around the hill and come back, I am asking you, not as a teacher but with affection as a friend genuinely concerned, what is your future? Even if you have already made up your mind to pass some exams and have a career, a good profession, you still have to ask, is that all? Even if you do have a good profession, perhaps a life that is fairly pleasant, you will have a lot of troubles, problems. If you have a family, what will be the future of your children? This is a question that you have to answer yourself and perhaps we can talk about it. You have to consider the future of your children, not just your own future, and you have to consider the future of humanity, forgetting that you are German, French, English, or Indian. Let us talk about it, but please realize I am not telling you what you should do. Only fools advise, so I am not entering into that category. I am just questioning in a friendly manner, which I hope you realize; I am not pushing you, directing you, persuading you. What is your future? Will you mature rapidly or slowly, gracefully, sensitively? Will you be mediocre, though you may be first class in your profession? You may excel, you may be very, very good at whatever you do, but I am talking of mediocrity of the mind, of the heart, mediocrity of your entire being.'

'Sir, I don't really know how to answer these questions. I have not given too much thought to it, but when you ask this question, whether I am to become like the rest of the world, mediocre, I certainly don't want to be that. I also realize the attraction of the world. I also see that part of me wants all that. I want to have some fun, some happy times, but the other side of me also sees the danger of all that, the difficulties, the urges, the temptations. So I really don't know where I will end up. And also, as you pointed out on several occasions, I don't know myself what I am. One thing is definite, I really don't want to be a mediocre person with a small mind and heart, though with a brain that may be extraordinarily clever. I may study books and acquire a great deal of knowledge, but I may still be a very limited, narrow person. Mediocrity, sir, is a very good word, which you have used, and when I look at it I am getting frightened—not of the word but of the whole implications of what you have shown. I really don't know, and perhaps in talking it over with you it may clear things up. I can't so easily talk with my parents. They probably have had the same problems as I have; they may be more mature physically, but they may be in the same position as I am. So if I may ask, sir, may I take another occasion, if you are willing, for you to talk with me? I really feel rather frightened, nervous, apprehensive of my capacity to meet all this, face it, go through it and not become a mediocre person.'

IT WAS ONE of those mornings that has never been before: the near meadow, the still beeches, and the lane that goes into the deeper wood—all was silence. There wasn't a bird chirping and the nearby horses were standing still. A morning like this, fresh, tender, is a rare thing. There is peace in this part of the land and everything was very quiet. There was that feeling, that sense of absolute silence. It was not a romantic sentimentalism, not poetic imagination. It was and is. A simple thing is all this is. The copper beeches this morning were full of splendour against the green fields stretching to the distance, and a cloud full of that morning light was floating lazily by. The sun was just coming up, there was great peace and a sense of adoration. Not the adoration of some god or imaginative deity but a reverence that is born of great beauty. This morning one could let go all the things one has gathered and be silent with the woods and the trees and the quiet lawn. The sky was a pale and tender blue and far away across the fields a cuckoo was calling, the wood pigeons were cooing, and the blackbirds began their morning song. In the distance you could hear a car going by. Probably when the heavens are so quiet with loveliness it will rain later on. It always does when the early morning is very clear. But this morning it was all very special, something that has never been before and could never be again.

'I am glad you have come of your own accord, without being invited, and perhaps if you are prepared, we can continue with our conversation about mediocrity and the future of your life. One can be excellent in one's career; we aren't saying that there is mediocrity in all professions; a good carpenter may not be mediocre in his work but in his daily, inward life, his life with his family, he may be. We both understand the meaning of that word now and we should investigate together the depth of that word. We are talking about inward mediocrity, psychological conflicts, problems and travail. There can be great scientists who yet inwardly lead a mediocre life. So what is going to be your life? In some ways you are a clever student, but for what will you use your brain? We are not talking about your career, that will come later; what we should be concerned about is the way you are going to live. Of course you are not going to be a criminal in the ordinary sense of that word. You are not, if you are wise, going to be a bully; they are too aggressive. You will probably get an excellent job, do excellent work in whatever you choose to do. So let us put that aside for a moment; but inside, what is your life? Inwardly, what is the future? Are you going to be like the rest of the world, always hunting pleasure, always troubled with a dozen psychological problems?'

'At present, sir, I have no problems, except the problems of passing examinations and the weariness of all that. Otherwise I seem to have no problems. There is a certain freedom. I feel happy, young. When I see all these old people I ask myself, am I going to end up like that? They seem to have had good careers or to have done something they wanted to do, but in spite of that they become dreary, dull, and they seem never to have excelled in the deeper qualities of the brain. I certainly don't want to be like that. It is not vanity, but I want to have something different. It is not an ambition. I want to have a good career and all that business, but I certainly in no way want to be like these old people who seem to have lost everything they like.'

'You may not want to be like them but life is a very demanding and cruel thing. It won't let you alone. You will have great pressure from society whether you live here or in America or in any other part of the world. You will be constantly urged to become like the rest, to become something of a hypocrite, say things you don't really mean, and if you do marry that may raise problems too. You must understand that life is a very complex affair—not just pursuing what you want to do and being pigheaded about it. These young people want to become something—lawyers, engineers, politicians, and so on; there is the urge, drive of ambition for power, money. That is what those old people whom you talk about have been through. They are worn out by constant conflict, by their desires. Look at it, look at the people around you. They are all in the same boat. Some leave the boat and wander endlessly and die. Some seek some peaceful corner of the earth and retire; some join a monastery, become monks of various kinds, taking desperate vows. The vast majority, millions and millions, lead a very small life, their horizon is very limited. They have their sorrows, their joys and they seem never to escape from them or understand them and go beyond. So again we ask each other, what is our future, specifically what is your future? Of course you are much too young to go into this question very deeply, for youth has nothing to do with the total comprehension of this question. You may be an agnostic; the young do not believe in anything, but as you grow older then you turn to some form of religious superstition, religious dogma, religious conviction. Religion is not an opiate, but man has made religion in his own image, blind comfort and therefore security. He has made religion into something totally unintelligent and impracticable, not something that you can live with. How old are you?'

'I'm going to be nineteen, sir. My grandmother has left me something when I am twenty-one and perhaps before I go to the university I can travel and look around. But I will always carry this question with me wherever I am, whatever my future. I may marry, probably I will, and have children, and so the great question arises— what is their future? I am somewhat aware of what the politicians are doing right throughout the world. It is an ugly business as far as I am concerned, so I think I won't be a politician. I'm pretty sure of that but I want a good job. I'd like to work with my hands and with my brain but the question will be how not to become a mediocre person like ninety-nine per cent of the world. So, sir, what am I to do? Oh, yes I am aware of churches and temples and all that; I am not attracted to them. I rather revolt against all that—the priests and the hierarchy of authority, but how am I going to prevent myself becoming an ordinary, average, mediocre person?'

'If I may suggest, never in any circumstances ask "how". When you use the word *how* you really want someone to tell you what to do, some guide, some system, somebody to lead you by the hand so that you lose your freedom, your capacity to observe, your own activities, your own thoughts, your own way of life. When you ask "how" you really become a second-hand human being; you lose integrity and also the innate honesty to look at yourself, to be what you are, and to go beyond and above what you are. Never, never ask the question "how". We are talking psychologically, of course. You have to ask "how" when you want to put a motor together or build a computer. You have to learn something about it from somebody. But to be psychologically free and original can only come about when you are aware of your own inward activities, watch what you are thinking, and never let one thought escape without observing the nature of it, the source of it. Observing, watching. One learns about oneself much more by watching than from books or from some psychologist or complicated, clever, erudite scholar or professor.

'It is going to be very difficult, my friend. It can tear you in many directions. There are a great many so-called temptations— biological, social, and you can be torn apart by the cruelty of society. Of course you are going to have to stand alone but that can come about not through force, determination, or desire but when you begin to see the false things around you and in yourself: the emotions, the hopes. When you begin to see that which is false, then there is the beginning of awareness, of intelligence. You have to be a light to yourself and it is one of the most difficult things in life.'

'Sir, you have made it all seem so very difficult, so very complex, so very awesome, frightening.'

'I am just pointing all this out to you. It doesn't mean that facts need frighten you. Facts are there to observe. If you observe them they never frighten you. Facts are not frightening. But if you want to avoid them, turn your back and run, then that is frightening. To stand, to see that what you have done may not have been totally correct, to live with the fact and not interpret the fact according to your pleasure or form of reaction, that is not frightening. Life isn't very simple. One can live simply, but life itself is vast, complex. It extends from horizon to horizon. You can live with few clothes or with one meal a day, but that is not simplicity. So be simple, don't live in a complicated way, contradictory and so on, just be simple inwardly. . . . You played tennis this morning. I was watching and you seem to be quite good at it. Perhaps we will meet again. That is up to you.'

'Thank you, sir.'

From Commentaries on Living Third Series, *Chapter 30*

Self-Interest Decays the Mind

Winding from one side of the valley to the other, the path crossed over a small bridge where the swiftly running water was brown from the recent rains. Turning north, it led on over gentle slopes to a secluded village. That village and its people were very poor. The dogs were mangy, and they would bark from a distance, never venturing near, their tails down, their heads held high, ready to run. Many goats were scattered about on the hillside, bleating, and eating the wild bushes. It was beautiful country, green, with blue hills. The bare granite projecting from the tops of the hills had been washed by the rains of countless centuries. These hills were not high, but they were very old, and against the blue sky they had a fantastic beauty, that strange loveliness of measureless time. They were like the temples that man builds to resemble them, in his longing to reach the heavens. But that evening, with the setting sun on them, these hills seemed very close. Far to the south a storm was gathering, and the lightning among the clouds gave a strange feeling to the land. The storm would break during the night; but the hills had stood through the storms of untold ages, and they would always be there, beyond all the toil and sorrow of man.

The villagers were returning to their homes, weary after a day's work in the fields. Soon you would see smoke rising from their huts as they prepared the evening meal. It wouldn't be much; and the children, waiting for their meal, would smile as you went by. They were large-eyed and shy of strangers, but they were friendly. Two little girls held small babies on their hips while their mothers were cooking; the babies would slip down, and get jerked up onto the hips again. Though only ten or twelve years old, these little girls were already used to holding babies; and they both smiled. The evening breeze was among the trees, and the cattle were being brought in for the night.

On that path there was now no other person, not even a lonely villager. The earth seemed suddenly empty, strangely quiet. The new, young moon was just over the dark hills. The breeze had stopped, not a leaf was stirring; everything was still, and the mind was completely alone. It wasn't lonely, isolated, enclosed within its own thought, but alone, untouched, uncontaminated. It wasn't aloof and distant, apart from the things of the earth. It was alone, and yet with everything; because it was alone, everything was of it. That which is separate knows itself as being separated; but this aloneness knew no separation, no division. The trees, the stream, the villager calling in the distance, were all within this aloneness. It was not an identification with man, with the earth, for all identification had utterly vanished. In this aloneness, the sense of the passing of time had ceased.

There were three of them, a father, his son, and a friend. The father must have been in his late fifties, the son in his thirties, and the friend was of uncertain age. The two older men were bald, but the son still had plenty of hair. He had a well-shaped head, a rather short nose, and wide-set eyes. His lips were restless, though he sat quietly enough. The father had seated himself behind his son and the friend, saying that he would take part in the talk if necessary, but otherwise would just watch and listen. A sparrow came to the open window and flew away again, frightened by so many people in the room. It knew that room, and would often perch on the window-sill, chirping softly, without fear.

'Though my father may not take part in the conversation', the son began, 'he wants to be in on it, for the problem is one that concerns us all. My mother would have come had she not been feeling so unwell, and she is looking forward to the report we shall make to her. We have read some of the things you have said and my father particularly has followed your talks from afar; but it is only within the last year or so that I have myself taken a real interest in what you are saying. Until recently, politics has absorbed the greater part of my interest and enthusiasm; but I have begun to see the immaturity of politics. The religious life is only for the maturing mind, and not for politicians and lawyers. I have been a fairly successful lawyer, but am a lawyer no longer, as I want to spend the remaining years of my life in something vastly more significant and worthwhile. I am speaking also for my friend, who wanted to accompany us when he heard we were coming here. You see, sir, our problem is the fact that we are all growing old. Even I, though still comparatively young, am coming to that period of life when time seems to fly, when one's days seem so short and death so near. Death, for the moment at least, is not a problem; but old age is.'

What do you mean by old age? Are you referring to the aging of the physical organism, or of the mind?

'The aging of the body is of course inevitable, it wears out through use and disease. But need the mind age and deteriorate?'

To think speculatively is futile and a waste of time. Is the deterioration of the mind a supposition, or an actual fact?

'It is a fact, sir. I am aware that my mind is growing old, tired; slow deterioration is taking place.'

Is this not also a problem with the young, though they may still be unaware of it? Their minds are even now set in a mould; their thought is already enclosed within a narrow pattern. But what do you mean when you say that your mind is growing old?

'It is not as pliable, as alert, as sensitive as it used to be. Its awareness is shrinking; its responses to the many challenges of life are increasingly from the storage of the past. It is deteriorating, functioning more and more within the limits of its own setting.'

Then what makes the mind deteriorate? It is self-protectiveness and resistance to change, is it not? Each one has a vested interest that he is consciously or unconsciously protecting, watching over, and not allowing anything to disturb.

'Do you mean a vested interest in property?'

Not only in property, but in relationships of every kind. Nothing can exist in isolation. Life is relationship; and the mind has a vested interest in its relationship to people, to ideas, and to things. This self-interest, and the refusal to bring about a fundamental revolution within itself, is the beginning of the mind's deterioration. Most minds are conservative, they resist changes Even the so-called revolutionary mind is conservative, for once it has gained its revolutionary success, it also resists change; the revolution itself becomes its vested interest.

Even though the mind, whether it be conservative or so-called revolutionary, may permit certain modifications on the fringes of its activities, it resists all change at the centre. Circumstances may compel it to yield, to adapt itself, with pain or with ease, to a different pattern; but the centre remains hard, and it is this centre that causes the deterioration of the mind.

'What do you mean by the centre?'

Don't you know? Are you seeking a description of it?

'No, sir, but through the description I may touch it, get the feeling of it.'

'Sir', put in the father, 'we may intellectually be aware of that centre, but actually most of us have never come face to face with it. I have myself seen it cunningly and subtly described in various books, but I have never really confronted it; and when you ask if we know it, I for one can only say that I don't. I only know the descriptions of it.'

'It is again our vested interest', added the friend, 'our deep-rooted desire for security, that prevents us from knowing that centre. I don't know my own son, though I have lived with him from infancy, and I know even less that which is much closer than my son. To know it one must look at it, observe it, listen to it, but I never do. I am always in a hurry; and when occasionally I do look at it, I am at odds with it.'

We are talking of the aging, the deteriorating mind. The mind is ever building the pattern of its own certainty, the security of its own interests; the words, the form, the expression may vary from time to time, from culture to culture, but the centre of self-interest remains. It is this centre that causes the mind to deteriorate, however outwardly alert and active it may be. This centre is not a fixed point, but various points within the mind, and so it is the mind itself. Improvement of the mind, or moving from one centre to another, does not banish these centres; discipline, suppression, or sublimation of one centre only establishes another in its place.

Now, what do we mean when we say we are alive?

'Ordinarily', replied the son, 'we consider ourselves alive when we talk, when we laugh, when there's sensation, when there's thought, activity, conflict, joy.'

So what we call living is acceptance or 'revolt' within the social pattern; it's a movement within the cage of the mind. Our life is an endless series of pains and pleasures, fears and frustrations, wanting and graspings; and when we do consider the mind's deterioration, and ask whether it's possible to put an end to it, our inquiry is also within the cage of the mind. Is this living?

'I'm afraid we know no other life', said the father. 'As we grow older, pleasures shrink while sorrows seem to increase; and if one is at all thoughtful, one is aware that one's mind is gradually deteriorating. The body inevitably grows old and knows decay; but how is one to prevent this aging of the mind?'

We lead a thoughtless life, and towards the end of it we begin to wonder why the mind decays, and how to arrest the process.

Surely, what matters is how we live our days, not only when we are young, but also in middle life, and during the declining years. The right kind of life demands of us far more intelligence than any vocation for earning a livelihood. Right thinking is essential for right living.

'What do you mean by right thinking?' asked the friend.

There's a vast difference, surely, between right thinking and right thought. Right thinking is constant awareness; right thought, on the other hand, is either conformity to a pattern set by society, or a reaction against society. Right thought is static, it is a process of grouping together certain concepts called ideals, and following them. Right thought inevitably builds up the authoritarian, hierarchical outlook and engenders respectability; whereas right thinking is awareness of the whole process of conformity, imitation, acceptance, revolt. Right thinking, unlike right thought, is not a thing to be achieved; it arises spontaneously with self-knowledge, which is the perception of the ways of the self. Right thinking cannot be learned from books or from another; it comes through the mind's awareness of itself in the action of relationship. But there can be no understanding of this action as long as the mind justifies or condemns it. So right thinking eliminates conflict and self-contradiction, which are the fundamental causes of the mind's deterioration.

'Is not conflict an essential part of life?' asked the son. 'If we did not struggle, we would merely vegetate.'

We think we are alive when we are caught up in the conflict of ambition, when we are driven by the compulsion of envy, when desire pushes us into action; but all this only leads to greater misery and confusion. Conflict increases self-centred activity, but the understanding of conflict comes about through right thinking.

'Unfortunately this process of struggle and misery, with some joy, is the only life we know', said the father. 'There are intimations of another kind of life, but they are few and far between. To go beyond this mess and find that other life is ever the object of our search.'

To search for what is beyond the actual is to be caught in illusion. Everyday existence, with its ambitions, envies, and so on, must be understood; but to understand it demands awareness, right thinking. There's no right thinking when thought starts with an assumption, a bias. Setting out with a conclusion, or looking for a preconceived answer, puts an end to right thinking; in fact, there is then no thinking at all. So right thinking is the foundation of righteousness.

'It seems to me', put in the son, 'that at least one of the factors in this whole problem of the mind's deterioration is the question of right occupation.'

What do you mean by right occupation?

'I have noticed, sir, that those who become wholly absorbed in some activity or profession soon forget themselves; they are too busy to think about themselves, which is a good thing.'

But isn't such absorption an escape from oneself? And to escape from oneself is wrong occupation; it is corrupting, it breeds enmity, division, and so on. Right occupation comes through the right kind of education, and with the understanding of oneself. Haven't you noticed that whatever the activity or profession, the self consciously or unconsciously uses it as a means for its own gratification, for the fulfilment of its ambition, or for the achievement of success in terms of power?

'That is so, unfortunately. We seem to use everything we touch for our own advancement.'

It is this self-interest, this constant self-advancement, that makes the mind petty; and though its activity be extensive, though it be occupied with politics, science, art, research, or what you will, there is a narrowing down of thinking, a shallowness that brings about deterioration, decay. Only when there's understanding of the totality of the mind, the unconscious as well as the conscious, is there a possibility of the mind's regeneration.

'Worldliness is the curse of the modern generation', said the father. 'It is carried away by the things of the world, and does not give thought to serious things.'

This generation is like other generations. Worldly things are not merely refrigerators, silk shirts, airplanes, television sets, and so on; they include ideals, the seeking of power whether personal or collective, and the desire to be secure, either in this world or the next. All this corrupts the mind and brings about its decay. The problem of deterioration is to be understood at the beginning, in one's youth, not at the period of physical decline.

'Does that mean there's no hope for us?'

Not at all. It's more arduous to stop the mind's deterioration at our age, that's all. To bring about a radical change in the ways of our life, there must be expanding awareness, and a great depth of feeling, which is love. With love everything is possible.

Sources and Acknowledgments

From the authentic report of the ninth public talk at Ojai, 9 July 1944, in *Collected Works of J. Krishnamurti,* © 1991 Krishnamurti Foundation of America.

From the authentic report of the second public talk at Ojai, 3 June 1945, in *Collected Works of J. Krishnamurti,* © 1991 Krishnamurti Foundation of America.

From the authentic report of the first public talk at Ojai, 27 May 1945, in *Collected Works of J. Krishnamurti,* © 1991 Krishnamurti Foundation of America.

From the verbatim report of the sixth public talk in Bangalore, 8 August 1948, in *Collected Works of J. Krishnamurti,* © 1991 Krishnamurti Foundation of America.

From the verbatim report of the fourth public talk at Ojai, 14 August 1955, in *Collected Works of J. Krishnamurti,* © 1992 Krishnamurti Foundation of America.

'Work', chapter 88 in *Commentaries on Living First Series,* © 1956 Krishnamurti Writings, Inc.

From 'Individual and Society', chapter 3 in *The First and Last Freedom,* © 1954 Krishnamurti Writings, Inc., © 1987 Krishnamurti Foundation of America.

From the verbatim report of the fifth public talk in Bombay, 24 February 1957, in *Collected Works of J. Krishnamurti,* © 1992 Krishnamurti Foundation of America.

'What Is the True Function of a Teacher?' chapter 31 in *Commentaries on Living Second Series,* © 1958 Krishnamurti Writings, Inc.

From the verbatim report of the sixth public talk at Varanasi, 12 January 1962, in *Collected Works of J. Krishnamurti,* © 1992 Krishnamurti Foundation of America.

'What Is Making You Dull?' chapter 17 in *Commentaries on Living Second Series,* © 1958 Krishnamurti Writings, Inc.

From chapter 17 in *This Matter of Culture,* © 1964 Krishnamurti Writings, Inc.

The verbatim report of the twelfth public talk in Bombay, 28 March 1948, in *Collected Works of J. Krishnamurti,* © 1991 Krishnamurti Foundation of America.

The verbatim report of the seventh public talk in Bangalore, 15 August 1948, in *Collected Works of J. Krishnamurti*, © 1991 Krishnamurti Foundation of America.

From the verbatim report of the eighth public talk in Poona, 17 October 1948, in *Collected Works of J. Krishnamurti*, © 1991 Krishnamurti Foundation of America.

From the verbatim report of the third public talk in Bombay, 26 February 1950, in *Collected Works of J. Krishnamurti*, © 1991 Krishnamurti Foundation of America.

'Beauty and the Artist', *The Urgency of Change*, © 1970 Krishnamurti Foundation London.

From the verbatim report of the tenth public talk in Bombay, 11 March 1953, in *Collected Works of J. Krishnamurti*, © 1991 Krishnamurti Foundation of America.

From the verbatim report of the thirteenth talk with students at Rajghat School, 20 January 1954, in *Collected Works of J. Krishnamurti*, © 1991 Krishnamurti Foundation of America.

From the verbatim report of the fourth public talk in Amsterdam, 23 May 1955, in *Collected Works of J. Krishnamurti*, © 1992 Krishnamurti Foundation of America.

From the transcript of the tape recording of the fourth public dialogue (with young people) at Saanen, 5 August 1972, © 1991 Krishnamurti Foundation Trust, Ltd.

'On Image Making', chapter 8 in *Krishnamurti on Education*, © 1974 Krishnamurti Foundation Trust, Ltd.

'Conditioning', chapter 2 in *Commentaries on Living Second Series*, © 1958 Krishnamurti Writings, Inc.

The transcript of the tape recording of the fifth public talk at Saanen, 24 July 1973, © 1991 Krishnamurti Foundation Trust, Ltd.

From the transcript of the tape recording of the third public dialogue at Saanen, 3 August 1973, © 1991 Krishnamurti Foundation Trust, Ltd.

'Right Livelihood', chapter 10 in *Truth and Actuality*, © 1977 Krishnamurti Foundation Trust, Ltd.

From the transcript of the tape recording of the second public talk at Ojai, 3 April 1977, © 1991 Krishnamurti Foundation Trust, Ltd.

'What Am I To Do?' chapter 48 in *Commentaries on Living Third Series*, © 1960 Krishnamurti Writings, Inc.

From *Letters to the Schools Volume One*, 1 December 1978, © 1981 Krishnamurti Foundation Trust, Ltd.

From chapter 7 in *This Matter of Culture*, © 1964 Krishnamurti Writings, Inc.

From *Letters to the Schools Volume One*, 15 December 1978, © 1981 Krishnamurti Foundation Trust, Ltd.